WAIST-HIGH IN THE WORLD

Voice Lessons:
On Becoming a (Woman) Writer

Ordinary Time:
Cycles in Marriage, Faith, and Renewal

Carnal Acts: Essays

Remembering the Bone House:
An Erotics of Place and Space

Plaintext: Deciphering a Woman's Life

In All the Rooms of the Yellow House (poems)

Waist-High in the World

A LIFE AMONG THE NONDISABLED

Nancy Mairs

BEACON PRESS

BOSTON

BEACON PRESS
25 Beacon Street
Boston, Massachusetts 02108-2892

BEACON PRESS BOOKS
are published under the auspices of
the Unitarian Universalist Association of Congregations.

01 00 99 98 97 96   8 7 6 5 4 3 2 1

Text design by Anne Chalmers
Composition by Wilsted & Taylor

Library of Congress Cataloging-in-Publication Data
can be found on page 214.

For
ANDREW HRYCYNA
enabler *par excellence*

There is only one question:
how to love this world.

—Mary Oliver, "Spring"

CONTENTS

HOME TRUTHS

Plunging In

I CANNOT begin to write this book. I've made some stabs at it, pried out of my rubbly brain a few pages, always "preliminary," from time to time. But mostly I write letters (never on time, so that the classic Nancy epistle always opens, "My apologies . . . "), or read material at least tangentially related to my subject, or merely play solitaire on my computer until I try my own patience to the point of despair.

The beginning of any project is always hard, I remind myself—the bigger, the harder—so that even a thousand-word review is initially daunting. But something more is dragging at my heels this time. That's purely a metaphorical cliché, of course. I haven't walked in years now, and even the jaws of the Hound of Hell haven't any force, unless I change the metaphor to "dragging at my wheels," in which case he could slow my progress considerably. But the automatic manner in which I came up with a comparison having so little to do with my real situation helps to explain my excessive dawdling. In embarking upon this book about disability, I have committed myself to spend months contemplating issues and experiences that mark mine as an undesirable, perhaps even an unlivable, life. True, no matter what I'm doing I can no longer forget that I have multiple sclerosis, but I can dull my awareness with books or beers or computer games. Writing has the opposite effect. It absorbs my attention utterly. And I don't *want* to think about my crippled life.

Then the telephone rings. "This is her husband speaking," I hear George say. We have chosen not to have an unlisted number, and whenever he's around he deftly fends off carpet cleaners and bankcard representatives and the hearty alumnae/i of one alma mater or another; I do the same in his absence; ours is a partnership of equals. "May I tell her who's calling?" He listens for a moment and then says, "Well, we're about to eat dinner, but I think she can give you a few minutes." This is no junk call. Bringing the telephone into the family room where I'm watching the NewsHour while he makes dinner, he tells me, "This is Jennifer, from Virginia. She's nineteen and she thinks she has symptoms."

The voice on the line has the high, tight, little-girl quality that the speech of many women takes on when they're fighting tears. She's a college student and she's just been reading one of my essays. She doesn't say which, but I assume that it's "On Being a Cripple" from

Plaintext, since that's the most widely anthologized. She hasn't even finished it yet, but she had to call as soon as she read about the blurred spot in my eye. At fourteen, she was treated for optic neuritis, which I recognize as a classic early symptom of MS, but she's never gotten an unequivocal diagnosis from a doctor. Or perhaps she has—a few are capable of forthrightness about this disease—but hasn't yet taken it in. Her new husband plainly hasn't, anyway, and so she is feeling isolated as well as scared.

"I'm pretty sure it's what I have," she winds up. "What do you think?"

I'm no neurologist, but she doesn't need a diagnosis. She's had plenty of diagnoses, too many and in conflict, as is so often the case with this baffling disease. Now she needs to talk herself into accepting the possibility that the doctors who have said "MS" are right, and as a stranger with no personal stake in her illness, I'm a safe audience. I let her talk.

"I'm sorry," she says at last. "Your husband said you're about to eat dinner. But I feel so much better just talking about MS. Maybe I could call again?"

"Of course. But maybe you should look for someone closer to home and save on the phone bill." We both laugh and say good-night.

George wasn't making up an excuse to keep Jennifer from talking too long. We really were about to have dinner. "You seem preoccupied," he comments as we eat our cheese tortollini. "Is it Jennifer?"

"Yes," I admit, meeting his smile. It goes on being Jennifer throughout the evening and into the dark, where I lie beside him with the black cat between us, the two of them sound asleep. I should have asked for her last name, I think, her address, her telephone number. Then I could . . . what? What am I supposed to do about Jennifer? Take away her MS, if that indeed is what she has? Failing that, calm her fears? Give her a college degree? Transform her husband, who will almost certainly leave her, and sooner rather than later, from a scared kid into a pillar of support and sympathy? I may wish I were God, but the truth is that I can't even tie my own shoes. Jennifer would be in real trouble if she had to rely on me to organize her life.

What I'm supposed to do about Jennifer, of course, is to write a book: one in which she can recognize and accept and even celebrate her circumstances, but also one that reveals to those who care about her what needs and feelings those circumstances may engender in her. Not a text about MS in particular or disability in general, because plenty of those exist. Not a little instruction book either, since practical training is best conducted one-on-one by physical and occupational therapists, and psychological advice to so diverse an audience could comprise only the most general platitudes. More like a Baedeker for a country to which no one travels willingly: the observations and responses of a single wayfarer who hopes, in sketching her own experiences, to make the terrain seem less alien, less perilous, and far more amusing than the myths and legends about it would suggest.

/ / /

Like Jennifer, I often need no more than someone to whom I can speak frankly about MS without being dismissed as a whiner (a distancing tactic often practiced by those in whom disability triggers unbearable anxiety), someone like my friend Joan. A nurse case manager who has worked with both the terminally and the chronically ill, Joan entered my life when I enrolled in a study to demonstrate the value to people with multiple sclerosis of regular support from nurses, social workers, and physical therapists. During our acquaintance, she has helped me in countless practical ways to prepare myself for George's possible death from cancer and my own relentless physical losses. But I have benefited most, I think, from her ears.

Who wouldn't? In a society that prates about, but seldom practices, communication, the craving to be listened to, heard, understood—which originates with the first terrified wail, the circling arms, the breast, the consolatory murmur—is hard to assuage. And because a cripple, in order to earn a shot at social intercourse with "normals,"[1] must never publicly lament her state, must preferably never even mention it, an other who treats disability as a safe topic of conversation offers immeasurable relief, as Jennifer's gratitude reveals.

Joan is a patient listener but hardly passive. She sits erect, eyes wide, hands loose in her lap, as though she didn't have several dozen others just like you whose stories she must soon rush off to hear. Every so often she interrupts with a brief question, which might be a request for information, or a signal that she's still with you no matter how tedious your tale, but almost never has so simple an effect. Usually, it startles me into new awareness, as when she asked, after I'd taken on at more than usual length one morning about the ways in which MS was cramping and skewing my life: "But Nancy, who would you be if you didn't have MS?"

Although I have known at least since freshman philosophy with dear, desiccated Holcomb Austin that such an intrinsically unanswerable question is not therefore imponderable, that it is, on the contrary, peculiarly and necessarily ponderable, I tend to duck rigorous duties of this sort in favor of working double-crostic puzzles, where I can count in time on laying out an answer—and only one, the right one—which, being of no consequence whatsoever, is powerless to disturb. Dozens of times, no doubt, I have let the question who I would be if I didn't have MS drift across my cerebral cortex and on out into the ether or wherever it is that spurned speculations go. But Joan's query, uttered in a high, soft voice nothing like my own, could not be so readily dismissed. It was given me, like a koan, to live with: not so much a question as a task.

Who would I be if I didn't have MS? Literally, no body. I am not "Nancy + MS," and no simple subtraction can render me whole. Nor do I contain MS, like a tumor that might be sliced out if only I could find a surgeon brave and deft enough to operate. Physiologically, lesions—sclerotic patches, or plaque, where the nerve sheath has been destroyed and scar tissue has formed in its place—have appeared throughout my brain and spinal cord:

they are integrated into my central nervous system just as thoroughly as the remaining healthy tissue. Since they can be located with Magnetic Resonance Imaging, I suppose they might be cut away, but what remained would be an even less serviceable version of a "Nancy" than the one MS has fabricated.

In an academic sense, this notion isn't difficult to grasp: that I would be somehow diminished, even damaged, without MS. But experientially, just the opposite seems true. That is, I often perceive myself to be living less authentically than other people. Whether I'd feel this way if I were congenitally disabled, or if my condition were not degenerative, I'm not sure; my perceptions may be shaped by a sense of contrast with the twenty-nine years I lived before diagnosis and by the bleak knowledge that, no matter how bad my symptoms are today, they will be worse tomorrow. How can I believe that my life is real when it feels so desperately provisional? Oddly, I don't consider the lives of other people with disabilities to be similarly inauthentic. Only my own seems flimsy and counterfeit.

Feeling thus deprived of a legitimate self, I can try to imagine an MS-less Nancy. And since writing has always formed the core of my identity, the means whereby I have saved and shaped my life, I wonder in particular whether I'd have become a writer if I hadn't developed this disease. In all likelihood, I would. From the age of thirteen I claimed writing to be my "future profession." But I could not conceivably have become the writer I am. Just as demyelinated lesions have spread throughout my central nervous system, their consequences have pervaded every region of my existence. MS is as much the essence of my "I" as my father's death and my mother's remarriage, my Yankee girlhood, my conversion to Roman Catholicism, my doctorate in English literature—some of these elements chosen, some arbitrarily handed to me. It can't be stripped away without mutilating the being who bears it.

Nevertheless, I might have chosen to write in such a way as to disregard or deny or disguise the fact that I have MS. In the process, I could have made a good many people happier than I have done, since the revelation of personal shortcomings (and chronic illness is definitely deemed a shortcoming) tends to rattle one's family members, especially the elderly ones, together with friends and even utter strangers who might be thought to have no stake in them at all. Moreover, I fondly suppose, I could have made a great deal more money, since many more readers are attracted to the carryings-on of bodies rising half-decomposed from the grave or tumbling half-clothed into an adulterous bed than to the quotidian truths of a body in trouble.

I could have. . . . I could have. . . . But I didn't. Why not? Because I have MS? Yes, I think so. My work has always been deliberately and deeply grounded in my own experience because that experience is all I reliably have that no other writer can give. There are readers—not a lot of them, perhaps, but even one is enough—who need, for a tangle of reasons, to be told that a life commonly held to be insufferable can be full and funny. I'm living the life. I can tell them.

What I cannot do, and would not choose to do even if I thought I could, is to depict and analyze "disability" as a global subject. The category is simply so broad, and the possible approaches to it so numerous, that all the attempts I've come across at generalizing about it run into difficulty. Theoretical books and articles do exist, though they are not always easy to track down, since the classification "disability studies" hasn't been widely adopted by bookstores, libraries, and indexes. In even the most ground-breaking and conscientious of these texts, however, like Barbara Hillyer's *Feminism and Disability*, the attempt to illuminate the subject as a whole tends to blur the focus and obscure significant distinctions. Then, too, by comparison with case studies, such as psychologist Ludwig Binswanger's "Case of Ellen West," and memoirs like *The Little Locksmith* by Katharine Butler Hathaway, the product of this global approach can make for dull reading. Yet many of the more personal accounts, though absorbing, concentrate so fully, almost claustrophobically, on the singularities of disabled life that they fail to reflect the ways in which such life is indistinguishable from any other sort: fueled by the same appetites, fraught with the same anxieties, replete with the same delights. My hope is that, in scrutinizing some of these elements common to the human condition—among them adjustment to change, body image and sexuality, the need for both independence and nurturance, the ceaseless search for equality and justice and pure pleasure—through the lens of my own experiences and those of people I know well, I can bring to life their particular significance in terms of disability.

At the outset, I want to make clear that I speak as an individual and not as a representative of "my kind," whatever you take that to be. The most acceptable designation for us just now seems to be "people with disabilities." One of the underlying problems with a comprehensive term like "disability," however, is that there has never been any universal agreement about who belongs in the company and who does not, or even what to call the presumed members. In a contest to give people like me a positive name, a man once won $50,000 for coming up with the term "people with differing abilities"—and the prize wasn't offered for the best phrase composed by a mentally impaired individual, either. Some other labels, marginally less vacuous though not necessarily more revelatory, include "handicapped" and its chipper variant "handi-capable," "physically challenged," and "developmentally delayed."

As one of my idiosyncrasies, I prefer to call myself a cripple. I have written elsewhere at length about this choice, for which I have very specific reasons. For one thing, because it is a word many people with disabilities find deeply offensive, I apply it only to myself, and so it reminds me that I am not speaking for others. For another, it lets you know what my condition is: I can't use my limbs as I once could. Blindness, deafness, intellectual impairment all qualify as "disabilities" (or "differing abilities" to people with mealy mouths), but the circumstances they impose are nothing like mine. "Mobility impaired," the euphemizers would call me, as though a surfeit of syllables could soften my reality. No such luck. I still can't sit up in bed, can't take an unaided step, can't dress myself, can't open doors (and I get damned sick of waiting in the loo until some other woman needs to pee and opens the door for me).

My choice may reflect a desire for accuracy more than anything else. In truth, although I am severely crippled, I am hardly disabled at all, since, thanks to technology and my relatively advantaged circumstances, I'm not prevented from engaging in the meaningful activities and relationships the human spirit craves. I'm not putting on a brave face here, and I'm not denying the seriousness of my situation. But I think it is very, very important to distinguish "disability," which is a social construct rather than a medical diagnosis, from some of the circumstances associated with it, often by people who have little direct knowledge of physical and mental limitations and their consequences. Like all negative terms, "disability" is part of a binary, existing in relation to a privileged opposite: that is, one is "disabled" only from the point of view of another defined by common social values as "able."

Binary thinking is merely a habit of mind, and despite the comfort of order and familiarity it offers, it doesn't apprehend reality, which is, let's face it, a frightful jumble. Gifts get handed out higgledy-piggledy. I'm so uncoordinated that,I'd never have gotten any good at tennis, even if I hadn't developed MS; but then, Monica Seles probably can't write her way out of a paper bag. (This is pure speculation, and it would serve me right if she won a Pulitzer some day.) From this perspective, the phrase "people with differing abilities," however uselessly inexact, intuitively grasps life's messiness in a way that the polarity "ability-disability" does not.

"I" am disabled, then, only from "your" point of view (and "you" from "mine"). Whoever gets to define ability puts everyone else in place, which (human nature tending to define one's own as the proper place) then becomes other, outside: a cheerless and chilly spot. No wonder I prefer the self-defined "cripple." When I have occasion to refer to a class with a broader spectrum of impairments, I use the more conventional "people with disabilities," or "the disabled" for short; and people who lack them I call "the nondisabled," since in relation to me, they are the deficient ones. Already, in this way, I begin to reconstruct the world.

I have spent most of my life among the nondisabled. At first, and for nearly three decades, I was simply one myself. Even after my multiple sclerosis was diagnosed, I didn't identify myself as disabled. True, a slight limp and crushing fatigue forced me to struggle through tasks that others accomplished with ease, but I carried them out nevertheless, and I may even have made them look easy sometimes. I didn't consciously avoid people with disabilities, but neither did I seek out their company; if I found myself in it, I was aware of being different from them, with their tremors, their slurred speech, their wandering eyes, their walkers and wheelchairs and leg bags. And that's the way I would have put it—"me" and "them"—a sign of the distance I perceived between us.

Today, I remain aware during every waking moment, and also in many of my dreams, that my legs don't work, that only one of my arms works (and that not very well), that my neck strains to hold up my heavy head, that my world is hemmed by walls to be banged, that the "them" from whom I'm now divorced are the nondisabled, bounding around heedlessly and hailing one another through the empty air above my head. Since I'm not about to abandon family and old friends, most of my activities still take place among them. I no longer avoid others with disabilities, however. In fact, one of the high points of my week is the water-exercise class sponsored by the MS Society, and not just because I can walk buoyed by water as I no longer can on dry land. A couple of weeks ago, a local television crew came to film our group.

"What do you suppose people will think when they see us?" asked Amy, paddling beside me with a long snake of neon-pink foam tucked under her arms for ballast.

"'Oh, the poor things!'" I laughed. "They have no idea we're capable of having fun." I looked around the pool. There was handsome Fritz, whose MS hardly shows except in his slightly halting gait. Joe was propped in the corner, head bobbing, wasted arms and legs churning the water. With the leg bag into which her catheter empties taped neatly in place, June, still pretty and stylish at sixty-eight, trailed a scent of expensive perfume above the stink of chlorine. Karen didn't have a leg bag, and her urine floated in its sealed pouch on the blue surface. Chip, though shy, joined in our laughter as we tried to stay upright while our feet traced a grapevine from one wall to the other. We weren't laughing at anything in particular. Our spirits were simply high. A stranger might see us as grotesque, I suppose. Once, I probably would have done so myself. Now, each week I see a group of friends lucky enough to be free at 11:00 on a Thursday morning for an hour of exercise.

These days, I "Tell all the Truth—," in accord with Emily Dickinson's instruction, "but tell it Slant—" more literally than Emily ever envisioned. Unless you've got a bad back, you're probably reading this sitting down. Look up from the page. Look around. Imagine that this is your angle of vision not just until you decide to get up and walk to the kitchen for a cup of coffee but forever. It's not a bad angle of vision, mind you (unless you want to check how much dust has accumulated on the top of the bookcase beside you), but it is a definite one, and the world you see from it is definitely different from the one you see when you're standing. This is my perpetual view, from the height of an erect adult's waist. And the difference has consequences. This is a book about such consequences.

In the past I have written out of my own experience about disability, but I have never examined the subject systematically. Nor have many other writers to my satisfaction. Yet increasingly sophisticated medical technology ensures that more of us who are born with or develop some sort of impairment will survive, living longer and more publicly than ever before. Life expectancy has increased more than thirty years since the turn of the century, a span that offers all kinds of new possibilities—among them, alas, the chance that illness or accident will permanently alter physical capacities. Thus, my interest in this subject, though intensely personal, is by no means private. Something without precedent is taking place, and we need a theoretical and imaginative framework for evaluating and managing the repercussions.

In writing a series of essays in which I explore the spatial and temporal exigencies of a life shaped by severe physical disability—a life bound by permissions (I have to weigh every act in terms of whether I can or cannot perform it) and obligations (I must overcome inertia to do the least thing)—I hope to discover what physical, emotional, moral, and spiritual elements shape the "differences" founded by disability. I begin with a welter of questions coalescing around several themes: language, rights, caregiving, bodies, the larger community. Then I ruminate. That's why I like the essay: it's contemplative, exploratory, even equivocal, not definitive. If there are absolute answers to the kinds of questions I can ask, I don't know them.

The essays in the first part of the book probe some of the intimate issues living with a disability raises. In the second part, I take up more public concerns. I have kept my focus throughout on the central and ambiguous reality of my title. I am literally diminished by my disability, reduced to a height of about 4' 8", consigned to gazing at navels (generally shrouded) other than my own. But diminution is not the whole of it. "Waist-high" also resonates with "knee-deep." This is no piteously deprived state I'm in down here but a rich, complicated, and utterly absorbing process of immersion in whatever the world has to offer.

This is not, however, a "feel-good" book. Too bad, because if it were, it might spend weeks on the *New York Times* best-seller list and make of me the wealthy woman I have always dreamed of being. In truth, I would give my eyeteeth (which narrowly escaped being knocked out along with my incisors when I fell flat on my face several years back) to write a best-seller, but this is not it. I am not now, nor have I ever been, a member of the inspirational class. I suppose you might call this instead a "feel-real" book, and reality has never been high on any popular list. I ask you to read this book, then, not to be uplifted, but to be lowered and steadied into what may be unfamiliar, but is not inhospitable, space. Sink down beside me, take my hand, and together we'll watch the waists of the world drift past.

Ups and Downs

IN THE winter of 1972, I began to struggle uphill. My aunt, the poet Jean Pedrick, held a workshop in her Beacon Hill home in those days; and although for the years since college I hadn't been able to compose anything except socially conscious and rather stridently righteous letters to various newspaper editors, I decided to join. One evening a week, instead of returning straight from work to my husband and two small children in our asbestos-shingled duplex in Boston's ugliest suburb, I took the subway from Harvard Square to Charles Street, walked along to Mount Vernon Street, and climbed almost to the crest, to number 48. This ascent, over worn and frost-heaved bricks often glazed with ice, is so steep that iron railings have been affixed on some of the weathered facades, and I began to grasp these just like one of those frail silver-haired dowagers, many of them still living on the Hill, who ventured out for Friday afternoon concerts at Symphony Hall, and for whom I'd always assumed the railings were designed.

Why didn't it seem odd to me that, at twenty-eight, I was behaving like an octagenarian? For one thing, I scarcely noticed, distracted as I was by the several and often conflicting tugs of career, family, poetic ambition, and a mounting obsession to escape the teeth-gritting cold and early dark. I did notice a little, though (else how could I remember?), but quickly explained my behavior away. True, I trembled with exhaustion by the time I reached Jean's fanlighted doorway, but I'd just put in an eight-hour day. At least once my left ankle turned painfully, but I was wearing high-heeled boots of soft brown suede, and perhaps they weren't laced tightly enough to stabilize my foot.

There were other signs to be explained or ignored. The lobby of the building at the Harvard Law School where I worked as a technical editor was paved with slate, and I started catching my toe on the slight irregularities in the floor's surface. I dropped lighted cigarettes from my left hand, and after a stretch of typing or knitting, my left fingers became so rubbery that I could hardly control them. A mysterious vertigo, diagnosed by the doctor as an "inner ear infection" then going around, kept me in a whirl for three weeks and then vanished. Earlier omens too, I can see now, much earlier, back at least to the fatigue that began to crush me in early adolescence. I couldn't swim as far or bicycle as fast as the other girls at summer camp. I dragged myself from class to class throughout high school and college, and later from home to office and back again. If I recognized these as signs of anything, they marked me as lazy, weak, and ungainly, and in my shame I flailed myself into more and more activity, hoping to develop both muscular and moral fiber.

So here I was, in pursuit of poetry, limp and half-reeling on Aunt Jean's doorstep. For years this had been my second home, in some ways dearer than whatever was my current first, and my heart lifted as I let myself in, crossed the hall past the wide stairway, its white balusters and dark handrail curving upward, and clattered down the narrower, darker stairwell beneath it into the basement kitchen, where Jean was stirring something redolent with last summer's herbs on the stove. It was a dim, low-ceilinged room, in contrast to the lofty pale-yellow living and dining rooms above, and the cooking together with the low embers in the little fireplace soon thawed my bones. We ate—Jean and I, her husband, and her two sons, whom I had helped care for from infancy but who now led enigmatic adolescent lives—at a round wooden table in a pool of syrupy lamplight.

When we had finished and washed the dishes, Jean and I went up to the wood-paneled library at the back of the house, where I took a pair of alabaster eggs down from a shelf and, cradling one in each hand for their soothing heft and smoothness, curled into the chair closest to the fire to await the other workshop members. There might have been a dozen. I've forgotten them now, except for Isador, a Russian émigré, elderly and elegant, with a beaked face and a drift of snowy hair, who wrote ambitious archaic verse, and James, perhaps eighteen, perhaps gay, who wrote a poem about green apples that stunned me with its plain grace. Crowded on chairs and the floor, we hunched over copies of each other's poems for a couple of hours and then dispersed into the icy night, not to see each other again for another week, strangers to one another's lives yet intimate at the root.

Jean's workshops, in which I have participated many times since, reflect her personality, short on posturing, long on kindness, and above all faithful to the work at hand; and under such conditions my confidence grew. In fact, during this period I first published a poem in something other than a school magazine. I must have used Jean's address, because I saw my author's copy for the first time at 48 Mount Vernon, standing at one end of the vast dining-room table while I held it for a very long time before I dared turn to the page supposed to bear—would it? did it? yes it did!—my name. "Prey" was a fine little poem, and although most of the others I wrote that winter were not, I began to believe that I could be a poet. The poem voiced my hatred of winter's bitterness, and it translated itself that year into a resolve to move someplace warm and work on a master's degree in creative writing.

I applied. I was accepted. And the following summer, on my twenty-ninth birthday, George and I loaded the children into a red Ford van named Ludwig and set out for Arizona.

My apprehension first surfaced on that day or one shortly before it when, clambering clumsily into the van, I said to George, "Once we get settled, I must find a doctor to look at my ankle." The reference was so off-hand that I doubt he took any note of it, and I gave it no more thought. Our lives were so bombarded by novelty! One little adventure after another: the rangy gray cat who showed up at our first picnic, accepting our humble offering of milk, olive loaf, and peanut-butter-and-jelly sandwich; the smoke that billowed from the engine cowling, which pell-melled the four of us into the sodden grass at the verge of the highway; the young hitchhiker who asked us to drive him to Kansas City but thought, on further consideration and after we'd bought him lunch, that he might as well come along all the way to Tucson (we thought not); the prodigious wind in Albuquerque that sucked and shoved at the canvas walls until sleeping in the tent felt like sleeping inside a giant lung; the glossy black bugs, bigger than field mice, that besieged us in a roadside toilet just after we crossed the state line into Arizona. Welcome to desert life!

Once we reached Tucson, at 10:30 on an August morning when the temperature was already 103° in the shade, there was an apartment to be rented and second-hand furniture to be bought, jobs to be secured, schools to be enrolled in. . . . What wonder that I forgot to take my funny foot to the doctor? About a month later, though, as I was crossing Speedway Boulevard with a new colleague in the creative writing program at the University of Arizona, he asked me whether I'd hurt my foot.

"No," I said, surprised. "Why?"

"You're limping."

Why had no one else ever commented on my gait? Had the limp appeared all at once? Probably not, although a summer of heat fiercer than any I'd experienced before might have exacerbated it. More likely, it developed so slowly that people who had known me for a long time grew used to it, and those who had just met me assumed that I'd always had it. Some must have wondered about it but been too "polite" to mention it. Our society promotes a kind of magical thinking, whereby some personal peculiarities, especially those implying dysfunction, can be effaced through studied inattention. In fact, I had been doing a fine job of ignoring my symptoms on my own. I have since been grateful that one "rude" man brought me up short. This moment marked—if any single one can be said to have done—the beginning of a new life, as I had wanted, but not the poet's life I believed myself to have embarked upon.

I stepped into it nonchalantly enough with a visit to the University of Arizona Student Health Service. This, I would later understand, must have jolted the amiable gray-haired doctor, in semi-retirement, who was accustomed to seeing strep throats and, no doubt, sexually transmitted diseases but not neurological catastrophe. After a silent and what seemed to me a cursory exam, he immediately got on the telephone to schedule an appointment with a neurologist.

"Can you even guess what the problem might be?" I asked him.

"No," he said firmly though not unkindly. "I can't."

You would think such a refusal would have unnerved

me utterly, but I don't recall that it did. I knew relatively little about medicine and nothing at all about neurology. I was young, in good health, without pain. My weak ankle was more a nuisance than anything else, if only because I had to walk considerable distances, in stunning heat, between my car, my office, and my classroom. When I wasn't memorizing Anglo-Saxon verbs or puzzling out abstraction ladders, I was house-hunting. In alien surroundings, knowing no one at all, George, the children, and I were trying to contrive a life that would suit us at least as well as the one we'd left on the other side of the country. I couldn't worry about one more thing.

For a few days, that is. Then I had to worry about a brain tumor. That's what the neurologist told me: the weakness on my left side, coupled with a history of headaches, pointed to a tumor, which a battery of tests would confirm and pinpoint. He would arrange for me to be hospitalized within a few days.

"I've always had a lot of psychosomatic ailments," I told him. "This is probably just one more."

"Not this time," he said firmly though not unkindly. "This time there's something in the right side of your brain that doesn't belong there."

Now I was well and truly terrified. As a girl, I had considered illness, even death, rather romantic—a view shaped, I suppose, by all those tragically tubercular heroines in the sentimental novels I devoured—and so I tended to dramatize my own maladies. Not that I made these up. I didn't have to. I routinely reeled through my life—head throbbing, vision blurred, stomach churning—until I had to surrender to bed in a darkened room for however many hours or days migraine claimed. Menstrual cramps, though less frequent, could be just as incapacitating, as, between last frost and first, could hay fever and the crusty weeping sores caused by poison ivy. I hated these symptoms, of course, but I secretly cherished them also, as signs of the delicate and high-strung nature suitable to an aspiring poet. A brain tumor, in those days, would probably have struck me as a seal of genius.

At twenty-nine, I had long since relinquished such fancies. Illness continued to plague me: headaches and cramps had been joined by colitis, triggering depression and panic attacks so severe that I had spent some months in a mental hospital a few years earlier. I was demonstrably delicate and high-strung, and these qualities had done nothing whatever to develop my poetic nature. On the contrary, they had bled away so much of my energy that at times I was hard pressed to create so much as a grocery list. I just wanted them to go away so that I could throw myself into the artistic life I was at last beginning to have the courage to grasp. Far from marking my genius, a brain tumor offered, quite literally, the kiss of death—tragic, without a doubt, but I wouldn't be around to savor its poignancy.

Over the span of several days, electrodes were pasted to my scalp, my spine and groin were punctured, dyes were injected and X rays taken, and in the event there simply was no brain tumor. This did not mean that there was no thing at all, the neurologist assured me. I had a "demyelinating syndrome of unknown etiology." If I'd been more medically sophisticated, I'd have recognized this as a code phrase for multiple sclerosis, the most common condition characterized by loss of myelin. As it was, several months passed before, having recognized my symptoms in an article in *Parade* magazine, of all places, I asked him, "Do I have multiple sclerosis?"

Probably, he told me, but only time would tell. He wasn't being cagey. These were the days before MS-specific neurological tests, CAT scans, and MRIs, and all he could do, after ruling out whatever else might be causing my weakness and fatigue, was wait for other symptoms typical of MS to appear. MS, a disease of the central nervous system (the white matter of the brain and the spinal cord), may affect any or all of its subsystems, each of which comprises a complex array of nerves controlling everything from whether your eyes can steadily follow a moving finger to whether your toes curl under when a sharp object scrapes along the sole of your foot. To be diagnosable, the disease must, more than once, cause discernible damage in more than one place in this vast constellation. The symptoms Dr. Buchsbaum initially observed were caused by an upper motor neuron lesion, that is, damage to the motor system; about eighteen months later, when an episode of optic neuritis signaled damage to quite a different system, the cranial nerves, he could confirm the diagnosis of MS.

So various are the possible symptoms that two people with the identical diagnosis may appear nothing alike. One may have the distinctive "scanning" speech pattern and erratic gait characteristic of lesions in the cerebellum; another, like me, may have no cerebellar involvement but be too weak to rise from a seat unassisted; still another may have transient episodes of blurred or double vision but otherwise demonstrate no symptoms at all. My disease manifested itself clearly enough so that the doctors didn't dismiss me as an hysteric or a malingerer, the lot endured, sometimes for years, by many with MS, especially those with the milder, relapsing-remitting form. I can't say I'm glad to have the chronic-progressive form instead, because the outlook is bleaker, but at least it spared me the emotional debilitation of being thought, or thinking myself, at least mildly deranged.

No one knows what causes MS. For some reason, perhaps in an aberrant response to an ordinary viral or bacterial infection, the immune system apparently begins to "think" of the myelin, the fatty substance that sheathes the nerves, as an alien invader to be destroyed. Without their protective coating, nerves short-circuit rather as electrical wires do, and when scar tissue forms where the myelin has been eaten away, signals can't get through at all. Since the details of this process continue to baffle researchers, they remain far from a cure, although a couple of drugs have showed promise in reducing attacks in relapsing-remitting MS. Still, because the disease can't be halted outright, it is invariably degenerative, although at widely differing rates.

And so, with this diagnosis, what had begun as an uphill struggle turned into a long slow slide downward, actually as well as metaphorically. People disabled traumatically—say, by a spinal cord injury sustained in an auto accident—have told me that they have an advantage because they know the worst from the outset, and any change can only be for the better. Others, congenitally disabled, claim that theirs is the easier lot because, never having known another way of being, they find their lives completely natural. I myself would contend that slow degeneration beginning in adulthood offers one time to grow incrementally into each loss and so more easily retain a modicum of composure throughout the process. None of these statements proves anything, of course, except the human tendency to put the best possible face on one's own experience, no matter how ghastly. Nevertheless, I persist in feeling grateful both that I lived nearly thirty years in the oblivion of "normalcy" and that I've had more than two decades to descend step by step (and then lurch by lurch) to the level where I live now.

Within the first year after those negative brain-tumor tests, I limped severely enough to require a cane for stability, but I managed with that until, five years later, I added a plastic brace (known as an ankle-foot orthosis, or AFO) so that I didn't trip over my own left toes. In the meantime, the blurry spot in my right eye that enabled Dr. Buchsbaum to diagnose MS caused me little trouble once I learned to look through it, rather as one peers through a raindrop on one's eyeglasses. In 1978, I first noticed symptoms suggesting that another upper motor neuron lesion was affecting my right side. Two years later, my range had decreased to the point that I adopted an Amigo, a small electric scooter, for all but short walks.

In 1986, I still felt competent to move to California for a stint of teaching at UCLA, where I lived alone, driving myself to school, shopping for my own food, cooking my own meals, washing my own laundry, emptying my own trash. Although a fall on my head right after my arrival gave me serious pause, I remained for seven months, and I returned to Tucson not for health reasons but in order to write a book. I loved this period in Los Angeles, my last of real, if limited, self-sufficiency. By the time the book was finished, I no longer had the stamina for a "real" job. Even though my limitation has proved a boon for my writing, providing time to concentrate intensely, I have regretted keenly the loss of income and identity that unemployment imposes.

I continued to travel alone, for readings and book-signings, until the summer of 1989, when, during six weeks at the School of Criticism and Theory at Dartmouth, I could feel my strength ebbing at an alarming rate. That autumn, beginning to fear that I'd put my foot on the brake pedal of my aging Volvo station wagon and nothing would happen, I gave up driving. Since renting a studio downtown thus became impractical, I moved my work into the tiny guest cottage behind our house. At the time of my fall in Los Angeles, I told myself that if I had another such mishap, I would know it was time to give up walking. I did fall several times thereafter, with no worse consequences than breaking my front teeth, but in August 1990 I knocked myself out cold on the floor of my family room. That was the signal I'd been waiting for. I've sat down ever since, trading in my scooter for a compact power wheelchair in 1992.

There's a just-the-facts-ma'am quality to such a rehearsal of losses that belies the anguish each of them has engendered. But anguish is, after all, a predictable response to loss of any kind. What has surprised me, all the way along, is how little self-pity I've felt. I don't take special credit for this. Given my historically histrionic streak, I would have expected to wallow in the stuff. Here I was, after all: an attractive young woman of intellectual and artistic promise, with dependent children and a vigorous husband, cut down, platitudinously enough, in my prime. Here I am now, a quarter of a century later, prime well past, hunched and twisted and powerless but for two twelve-volt batteries beneath my ass. Woe is me!

Except that, on the whole, woe *isn't* me. I don't think I am, as the recovery movement would have it, "in denial" (perhaps because I'll never be "in recovery"). I feel—and feel fully—the ordinary complement of negative emotions in response to specific triggers: anger and frustration at my clumsiness; embarrassment about my leaky bladder; wistfulness for the dancing and hiking and cycling I'll never do again; guilt that my helplessness burdens family and friends; anxiety about further deterioration. I simply don't feel especially sorry for myself. Neither do most of the other people with disabilities I know, so I'm neither unusually brave nor exceptionally thick-skinned. Self-pity is simply one of those sentiments more likely to be projected onto one from the outside than generated within. That is, because nondisabled people pity us, they presume that we must also pity ourselves. This supposition may actually function as a powerful antidote, inasmuch as almost every cripple I know, sensing it every day, resents and actively repudiates it.

Most nondisabled people, except perhaps the very old, have gotten the message that it isn't exactly politically correct to look me up and down and burst out, "Oh, you poor thing! I feel so sorry for you!" Instead, their response tends to take the form of unmerited admiration. "You are so brave!" they gush, generally when I have done nothing more awesome than to roll up to the dairy case and select a carton of vanilla yogurt. "I could never do what you do!" Of course they could—and likely would—do exactly what I do, maybe do it better, but the very thought of ever being like me so horrifies them that they can't permit themselves to put themselves on my wheels even for an instant. Admiration, masking a queasy pity and fear, serves as a distancing mechanism, in other words. Better to deny the perfectly ordinary qualities most cripples possess, thus ascribing to them an other, safely remote reality, than to risk identification of their own lives with a life that dismays and perhaps even disgusts them.

God knows most cripples never want for authentic courage to confront the obstacles in their lives—don't get me wrong—and it is the sense of rising to a challenge that provides the best corrective to self-pity I know. Elsewhere, I have written disparagingly of the use of "physically challenged," among other euphemisms, to designate people with disabilities. (Of course, as the first sentence in this paragraph reveals, I'm not that wild about "people with disabilities" either.) I continue to reject it, because I think it blurs the distinction that makes us unique: we are not the only "physically challenged" beings, as any marathon runner will tell you, but we are the only ones whose bodies don't work in the ways they were plainly formed to do. In repudiating the euphemism, however, I do not dismiss either the fact or the value of challenge itself.

The bare rehearsal of my progressive disability conceals an increasingly intricate set of exercises in problem-solving that have kept me on my toes (even though off my feet) for nearly a quarter of a century. What to do when sacks of groceries became too heavy to carry? Ask the clerk to pack more of them with fewer items. What to do when I got too weak to carry them at all? Buy a little four-wheeled wire cart. What to do when I could no longer push the cart? Request that someone else carry them to the car. What to do when I could no longer drive to the market in the first place? Have George take me. What if George should get too busy or too ill? Reserve a ride on Van Tran; the driver will carry my parcels into the house. What if I no longer have the strength to put my own groceries away or to go out at all? Hire a shopping service.

Virtually every activity, no matter how automatically most people would carry it out, has necessitated for me this sort of attention, resourcefulness, and adaptability. Like many young women of my generation, the first to aspire to "have it all," I vastly overextended myself when I was younger, and by the time of my diagnosis, I wore so many hats I could hardly hold my head up: wife, mother, teacher, graduate student, political activist, not to mention cook, housekeeper, family correspondent, redecorator, needlewoman, digger of pet graves. . . . Over the years, I've had to pare back this list; and relinquishing, or at least revising, each role has wounded and shamed me.

When my children were growing up, for instance, I was often wracked by guilt that they didn't have a "normal" mother. I was convinced, in fact, that my disability was traumatizing them. Such arrogance! This was considerably deflated when, as adults asked to reflect on being raised by a cripple, Anne and Matthew were all but nonchalant. "How should I explain the differences between my upbringing and a more 'normal' one, when this is all I have known?" Matthew asked. "From my point of view it isn't anything extraordinary; quite the opposite in fact." Recalling how, over time, she stopped functioning as my sous-chef and I became hers, Anne said, "Because this change in our roles was so gradual, it seemed natural to me. I never seriously rebelled against the increasing demands on me, even as a moody sensitive teenager."

Of course, they have regrets. "One thing I remember being particularly pained about while growing up," Anne said, "was Mom's eventual inability to join Matthew, Dad, and me on camping trips. Camping was my favorite family activity. But after Mom was diagnosed with MS, the trips became less frequent. When we did go camping, instead of joining us on a hike through the woods, Mom would have to stay at the campsite reading. Later she begged off camping trips entirely, leaving Dad, Matthew, and me to go alone. I felt disappointed by her abandonment, but I doubt I ever strongly expressed it; how could I complain when she was the one who had to stay home? These occasions when Mom couldn't join the rest of us were the only times I remember feeling really angry at the disease for keeping Mom from us."

In general, their memories of the period when I supposed myself to be destroying their happy childhoods are remarkably sunny, like this one of Matthew's: "We used to regularly take outings to the Desert Museum. Although Mom could still walk, the miles involved in trekking around that place were more than she could really handle, and so we were using a chair. I had fun pushing the chair, I was maybe even a little possessive of it, and despite my pushing at what I'm sure, in retrospect, was an uncomfortable rate of speed, she would always ask if I wanted to push it. A mother's love that, eh? She had several choices for more comfortable rides, but because her mad son loved to do it, she asked him to. So you call my mother disabled? Pray tell, how? What important ability does she lack?"

In short, I appear to have been an adequate mother. I was not always an adequate wife. George recalls, "I used to have dreams of Nancy slipping away. She would go no matter how I hung on." He was the one who slipped away, though, from my arms into those of another, healthier woman, and he attributes this infidelity in large measure to my MS. During whatever hours he could steal with Sandra, he could forget about me entirely, becoming the single, carefree, sexy youth he yearned—as who does not at times?—to be. In the end, because of his own illness, he abandoned this refuge; but at least he learned that remaining with me is his choice. Even now, he confesses, "I can imagine leaving. Perhaps at some point I will leave. But now I don't feel like it."

Although my motherly guilt has long since been allayed by the success with which Matthew and Anne grew up despite my lacks, and although George and I now live together, however provisionally, in harmony, I still sometimes wallow in remorse for my own shortcomings. "Comparisons are odious" was one of the truisms by which my mother raised me, but I never quite took this lesson to heart. I look at other women my age, and often much older, racing from kitchen to office to supermarket to fitness center to political meeting, and my own undertakings seem trifling and drab. Knowing that haste depletes me dangerously, I try to schedule only one major activity in a day, allowing ample time to prepare for it ahead of time and to decompress afterward. Living just blocks from a major intersection, I can hear the muffled sounds of traffic. People are taking their paychecks to Saguaro Credit Union and dropping off their clothes at Sparkle Cleaners and popping into 7–Eleven for a newspaper on their way home, just as I once did. The world is going on out there, altogether too nicely, without me.

Now that my own racing around has ended, I have had to learn to take satisfaction in stasis, or else drive myself mad with regret and boredom. I'm always especially aware of my hard-won patience when George and I travel, because then we use a manual wheelchair, and whenever George must go off on an errand, I am fixed in one spot. Possessing a Zen disposition himself, he has an unfortunate propensity for parking me squarely in front of massive concrete pillars in airports. If I can persuade him to turn me outward to the world, I can entertain myself for long moments by contemplating the queer choices people make in traveling costumes, imagining the stories behind the encounters and conversations of strangers, or flirting with small children. You may well have hurtled past, in Denver or Des Moines, in Seattle or Salt Lake City or Sacramento, never noticing me down here; but I, no doubt, have seen you.

The languid, pensive state in which I now live much of the time has calmed me and expanded my contentment immeasurably. Because my slightest gesture requires effort now, I must focus on each moment, without much regard for past mistakes or the future's threats or blandishments. Over the years, I have grown accustomed to performing every action as if for the last time. Of course, it may not truly be the last time; and when it is, I won't know so for sure until later; so I assuage regret by saying farewell as I go. I don't actually remember the final time that, having plummeted to the floor, I dragged myself upright again, but since, toward the end, I did so fully aware that I might never have another chance, I feel satisfied that I honored this ability just as long as it was mine.

Relaxed and focused, I feel emotionally far more "up" than I generally did when I stood on two sound legs. Nondisabled people, I find, tend to be skeptical of such contentment. A couple of weeks ago, a friend ringing me up to ask if she could come over to lunch opened with the conventional "How are you?"

"Just fine!" I said.

Apparently I spoke with enthusiasm, because she responded, startled, "How can you *say* that?"

"I don't know, Barrie," I laughed. "I guess it must be true."

"You're really amazing," she said. I didn't argue. She is, after all, entitled to her own feelings of amazement. From my perspective, however, I was simply having a good day. I have those, just like normal people.

For the most part—and you can believe this or not as you choose—I consider my life unusually privileged. How many people get to adapt themselves deliberately to their circumstances? How many get to adopt a pace that suits them—or even have a chance to puzzle out what that pace might be? How many get to devote themselves fully to the pursuits that most delight them: in my case, observing, reflecting, conversing, writing? How many cherish what little they have on any given day, in the full knowledge that on some tomorrow it will inevitably be less?

Here I am today: the white matter of my brain is shot to hell, but as my doctor told me after I finally had an MRI a couple of years ago, my cortex is beautiful! This was terrific news to me, because if I have to go through this experience, I want to be able at least to think about it. Almost equally important to me, my speech has not yet been affected, so I can still give readings from my work. Except for the scotoma in my right eye and the normal effects of aging, my vision is good. Since the neurological damage affects my motor system almost exclusively, I can still sense pain, temperature, and light touch, and I am free of tremors. From a seated position, I can pull myself to my feet and stand for short periods with assistance, although I can no longer take a step. My left arm and hand don't work at all; my right ones still have some strength. Certainly I am not mobility impaired; in fact, in my Quickie P100 with two twelve-volt batteries, I can shop till you drop at any mall you designate, I promise. George can drive me in a van with a lift; and when he's not available, Tucson offers door-to-door service via Van Tran for $1.20 each way. I have a computer with voice-activated software and a speaker telephone for my work. A housekeeper cleans my living space and my clothes. Most of the time, George provides me fabulous food, but in a pinch, there's always Pizza Hut.

Where will I go from here? Down: only down, until one day I am prostrate, and perhaps further still, however that can be. That is the nature of my corporeality. Will my spirits flag as my life goes steadily flatter, in every sense of the word? Perhaps. All I know is that I have already slid much further than I ever thought I could bear to do; and so far, so good.

Body in Trouble

"CONCEPTUALIZE the body," I was instructed by the organizers of a conference at which I had been invited to speak a couple of years ago, and I balked. Something was wrong with this syntax, as though I myself—my thinking self—were no body, as though this disembodied self could speak not only for the body that it is not but for bodies in general (presumably human ones, though nothing in the directive actually debarred my corpulent corgi from my deliberations). The effect of the assignment seemed to me to divorce the speaking subject from her own corporal existence while permitting her to make free, in the chastest of senses, with the bodies of others. But why did my lecture topic—not at all an odd one at a feminist conference—strike me as so problematic?

I was squeamish about grammar in this case for at least a couple of reasons, both of which have to do with my reality as a body who has been in trouble of one sort or another for almost as long as I can remember. The first is that this construction reinforces the age-old Western dichotomy between mind, active and in control, and body, that wayward slug with which it is afflicted. Sheer knowledge of our bodies has helped dispel that myth. Before advances in medical technology began permitting us to illuminate and scrutinize our mysterious mute inner reaches, the terrain beneath the skin might well have seemed alien, even wholly separate from our "true" being. No longer. Recently, when an intestinal disturbance required my husband to have a colonoscopy, I sat in the corner and watched on a television screen as a minute camera zoomed through the glistening roseate chambers of his large bowel, thereby becoming one of the few women in the world who can truly profess that she knows and loves her partner both inside and out. In fact, since George slept through the whole procedure, I can now claim to know him more fully than he knows himself.

Over the years, as George's melanoma has moved from his skin through his lymphatic system into his belly, necessitating surgery and then chemotherapy, and as my multiple sclerosis has immobilized me, we have had to come to terms with ourselves as bodies. The physical processes of a perfectly healthy person may impinge so little on her sense of well-being that she may believe herself separate from and even in control of them. From here it's a short leap to the conviction that cerebral phenomena are of a different, generally higher, order than other bodily events and thus possess transcendent and even immortal qualities, at which point the imagined mind becomes the even more fantastic soul.

The body in trouble, becoming both a warier and a humbler creature, is more apt to experience herself all of a piece: a biochemical dynamo cranking out consciousness much as it generates platelets, feces, or reproductive cells to ensure the manufacture of new dynamos. When it became clear that the somatic basis of the depressive symptoms that had plagued me since adolescence required sustained biochemical intervention, I resisted.

"But I won't be myself if I have to take drugs!" I wailed to my therapist.

"I think," he replied, "that you're more yourself when you're medicated than when you're not." I had no self, I finally recognized, apart from my brain chemistry, but with it I had my choice of two: the self who starved and lay awake night after night and spent every conscious minute trying to postpone suicide, or the self who swallowed her pills and got on with her life. I am in every way, in my dreams as in my waking, the creature of my biochemistry. The body alone conceptualizes the body, conferring upon it, among other dubious endowments, a "mind."

But whose body? My second misgiving about my task arose from the two ways in which the phrase "the body" may be read: one reduces the speaker's flesh to a thing ("the body," not the true me), and the second suggests that one can universalize bodily experiences that may be in reality entirely idiosyncratic ("the body," not mine necessarily). For years after I began to have symptoms of MS, I used language to avoid owning them: "The left hand doesn't work anymore," I said. "There's a blurred spot in the right eye." In distancing myself from my ravaged central nervous system, I kept grief at bay; but I also banished any possibility of self-love. Only gradually have I schooled myself to speak of "my" hands, "my" eyes, thereby taking responsibility for them, though loving them ordinarily remains beyond me.

So, then: my body. And only my body. The specificity of the personal pronoun is critical to me (and to this book) because the range of bodies with disabilities is so exceptionally broad that I could not possibly speak for them all and do not wish to be perceived as trying to do so. This problem exists for any population, of course, as white middle-class academic feminists rapidly found out when they began to generalize about women, but the label "disability" masks a diversity of even more incomparable lives. What in my experience has prepared me to portray the realities of an old woman with Alzheimer's, even though we are both female; or a teenager with muscular dystrophy, even though neither of us can walk; or a young man with schizophrenia, even though I too have been confined to a mental hospital; or my niece whose eyes were removed when she was ten, even though we are blood kin? I would not presume to conceptualize their bodies. I can only represent my own experience as authentically as the tricks and vagaries of language will permit, trusting others to determine what similarities we share and make use of them as they see fit.

Here is my troubled body, dreaming myself into life: a guttering candle in a mound of melted wax, or a bruised pear, ripe beyond palatability, ready for the compost heap. The images, though they vary, always bear the whiff of spoliation. If there ever was a time of unalloyed love, I have long forgotten it, though I had hopes in early adolescence: that my breasts would grow magically larger and my mouth magically smaller; that I would become a strong swimmer and sailor and cyclist; that men, irresistably drawn, would touch me and I'd burst into flame. Mostly I was, as I was trained to be, disappointed in myself. Even in the fifties, before the dazzle of shopping malls and the soft pornography of advertising for every product from fragrance to bed linen, a girl learned to compare herself unfavorably to an ideal flashed at her on glossy magazine covers and cinema screens and then to take measures to rectify her all too glaring deficiencies. I started painting my lips with Tangée when I was eleven, polishing my fingernails as soon as I stopped biting them, for my first great love at thirteen, plucking my eyebrows and wearing green eyeshadow at sixteen. I strapped on padded bras and squeezed into pantiegirdles to ac-centuate the positive and e-liminate the negative. I could not imagine a body that didn't require at least minor structural modification.

I still can't, and neither can any other woman I know.

Not long ago, my mother and I shared a mirror as we put on faces for a festive evening. "I hate these," she said, drawing her fingers down the lines from the corners of her mouth, "and this," patting the soft sag of flesh under her chin. I didn't try to protest, though she is a pretty woman, because I hate the same features now developing in my own face. One sister's breasts hang down, she laments, and the other's hips are too broad; my mother-in-law's bosom is too ample; even my daughter, possessed of a body too shapely for complaint, rues her small round nose. All these women, ranging in age from thirty to eighty-four, are active and fit, and fortunately they are too absorbed by their demanding lives to dwell upon whatever defects they perceive themselves to display. None could be considered vain. Not one has mutilated herself with rhinoplasty or liposuction or any of the other measures cosmetic surgeons have developed for emptying women's pockets into their own. Their dissatisfaction with their bodies seems as natural to them as their menses or hot flashes, simply an element of womanly existence.

Even if I hadn't developed MS, then, I would probably view myself with some distaste. But by the time I was thirty, I walked with a limp and used a cane. By forty, I wore a brace on my left leg and used a motorized scooter to cover all but short distances. Now, in my fifties, I divide my time between wheelchair and bed, my belly and feet are swollen from forced inactivity, my shoulders slump, and one of my arms is falling out of its socket.

The other day, when my husband opened a closet

door, I glimpsed myself in the mirror recently installed there. "Eek," I squealed, "a cripple!" I was laughing, but as is usually the case, my humor betrayed a deeper, darker reaction. We have almost as many mirrors as a fun house, to give our small quarters an illusion of space, but I avoid looking into them straight on, and I dislike the objective evidence of photos as well. ("If I don't see you," my sister used to tease, her hands over her eyes, "you can't be you!") I love my wheelchair, a compact electric model called a Quickie P100, and I've spent so much time in it, and become so adept at maneuvering it, that I have literally incorporated it—made it part of my body—and its least ailment sends me into a greater tizzy than my own headaches. But the wheelchair I experience is not "out there" for me to observe, any more than the rest of my body is, and I'm invariably shocked at the sight of myself hunched in its black framework of aluminum and plastic.

Although—or perhaps because—I am appalled by my own appearance, I devote an absurd amount of time and expense to its decoration. "Not for Mom peignoirs and pillows as she takes to her bed," my daughter points out. "No, she still likes to get out and find just the right color turtleneck or the perfect pair of black leggings." The green eyeshadow of youth has proliferated into every color of the rainbow, as well as a number that don't appear there, and been joined by foundation, mascara, blusher, and lipstick, not to mention the creams and lotions used to prepare the relentlessly wrinkling surface for this palette. I dread the day when my fingers become so weak that I have to go into the world with my bare face hanging out.

Already I can no longer dress myself, and I quip about moving to a climate so temperate that I wouldn't need any clothing at all, but in truth, of course, I could bear to hang out my bare body even less than my bare face. I buy garment after garment in the hope of finding one that will fit well enough to clothe me in some tatter of grace. Designers conceive tall bony pubescent bodies swinging down runways to some hectic beat on skinny but serviceable legs, and even the apparel that makes it to the outlet stores where I shop is cut for a lithe erect form in motion. This is who I want to be, of course, and so I cruise the aisles searching for a magic cloak that will transform me into her.

The "her" I never was and am not now and never will become. In order to function as the body I am, I must forswear her, seductive though she may be, or make myself mad with self-loathing. In this project, I get virtually no cultural encouragement. Illness and deformity, instead of being thought of as human variants, the consequence of cosmic bad luck, have invariably been portrayed as deviations from the fully human condition, brought on by personal failing or by divine judgment. The afflicted body is never simply that—a creature that suffers, as all creatures suffer from time to time. Rather, it is thought to be "broken," and thus to have lost its original usefulness; or "embattled," and thus in need of militaristic response, its own or someone else's, to whip it back into shape; or "spoiled," and thus a potential menace to the bodies around it. In any case, it is not the sort of thing your average citizen would like to wake up next to tomorrow morning.

To embrace such a self requires a sense of permission some people achieve more readily than others. George's body, like mine, has been battered by aging and illness. Liver spots have appeared on the backs of his hands and crow's feet at the corners of his eyes and white hairs in his beard. He bears a puckered scar on his right upper arm. A second scar, in his right armpit, is invisible, but his right breast sags where the muscles were severed. A third runs the length of his abdomen; the surgeon boasted of his handiwork, but frankly George's reconstructed navel looks a little improvised. For several years now he has been impotent, and although I miss his erections sadly, he does not. "I'm at peace with my body," he says. I am at a loss to explain his complacency except as the habit of a lifetime of believing that whatever way he is is as he ought to be, a confidence that seems to arise in part from the possession of a penis, whether that organ itself still rises or does not. He senses himself to be "all right," revising his self-image as necessary to maintain this equilibrium, just as reflexively as I feel myself to be "all wrong."

In fact, he is also at peace with my body in a way that I am not. He always has been, and now that I can do little for myself, he rubs in lotion and sprays on scent, clips nails and stray hairs, wrestles stockings onto my rubbery legs, lifts me off toilets in women's rooms from

Los Angeles to London. His ministrations, combining skill with sensuality, reassure me that this is the body he has loved since he first set eyes (or, if recent research is correct, nose) on it thirty-five years ago. Not long ago, a young clerk in a Victoria's Secret shop, joining in our deliberations over assorted styles and colors of underpants, was clearly startled by George's experienced and critical eye. Settling on a couple of briefs, in a sensible cut but a sexy fabric, he explained that he was the one who had to get me into them, but she still seemed to find his expertise—so patently nonprurient, rather like my grandmother's—a little kinky. Which was, he'd doubtless point out, her problem, not his. The peace he feels with his body has rendered him secure enough in his sexual identity that he enters and exits feminine space with aplomb. George's attentive and affectionate presence provides proof against the revulsion with which I am all too apt to greet myself; and even his easier peace depends in part, I am sure, on the fact that my body has remained crazy about his body throughout its vicissitudes.

I doubt that any body, whether in trouble or out, can fully conceive a self without an other to stroke it—with fingertips and lips, with words and laughter—into being and well-being. Research has demonstrated that infants deprived of touch fail to thrive, and that blood pressure is lowered and spirits are raised in elderly people given pets to caress. If physical stimulation is wholesome—even lifesaving—at the extremes of life, why should we suppose the middle to be any different?

Our bodies conceptualize not only themselves but also each other, murmuring: Yes, you are there; yes, you are you; yes, you can love and be loved.

I have been fortunate, as many people with disabilities are not, to have had throughout my adult life someone who loves me into being in just this way. Recently, when George and I were sharing memories of a friend with rheumatoid arthritis who had just died unexpectedly, I recalled an April morning years ago at the school where the three of us, close contemporaries, were teaching. "It's spring," Jill sighed as she thumped into the chair beside mine in the faculty room. "How I wish I had someone to love!" I was startled by this revelation. Still newly and mildly disabled myself, I hadn't yet given much thought to the sexual predicament in which a crippled body may find herself. Jill had developed arthritic symptoms in infancy, although not until she was in college did the damage to her joints really limit her mobility. She might not have been a pretty woman even without arthritis; as it was, she had the receding chin and twisted fingers characteristic of this disease, together with the "moon" face caused by anti-inflammatory drugs, and she moved slowly, stiff-legged, on crutches. Outgoing and energetic, she could on occasion overwhelm those around her with criticisms or demands, but despite her prickliness, she was warm and funny and had many devoted friends. I don't suppose she ever had the lover she wished for, though.

Desire depends very little on physical perfection or prowess. Desirability, alas, depends on these a great deal. Perhaps the sociobiologists are correct in theorizing that we are attracted to those who appear most fit for reproduction; or perhaps we merely want whatever we are trained to want. Regardless of origin, standards of beauty and sources of arousal may vary from culture to culture, but every culture has them; and ours, at least, rigorously excludes most physical defects. A man with a slight limp or a patch over one eye, suggesting a wound from some heroic action, might still be considered dashing (though so many years have passed since the last "honorable" war that this effect may have worn off), but if he requires a wheelchair or a guide dog, he is likely to be viewed as a problem rather than a sex object. And although a condition that doesn't cause outright disfigurement, such as deafness, may be tolerated in a woman, I can't think of a single sign of injury or illness that would actually confer cachet.

On the contrary, the general assumption, even among those who might be expected to know better, is that people with disabilities are out of the sexual running. Not one of my doctors, for example, has ever asked me about my sex life. Most people, in fact, deal with the discomfort and even distaste that a misshapen body arouses by dissociating that body from sexuality in reverie and practice. "They" can't possibly do it, the thinking goes; therefore, "they" mustn't even want it; and that is *that*. The matter is closed before a word is uttered. People with disabilities can grow so used to unstated messages of consent and prohibition that they no longer "hear" them as coming from the outside, any more than the messengers know they are "speaking" them. This vast conspiracy of silence surrounding the sexuality of the disabled consigns countless numbers to sexual uncertainty and disappointment.

Many years ago, I concluded an essay called "On Not Liking Sex" with the speculation that I might one day write another on liking sex. This, I guess, constitutes that long-deferred essay. I really do like sex. A lot. Especially now that the issues of power and privacy that vexed me then have resolved themselves with time. Unfortunately, I like intercourse best of all, and the knowledge that I will never experience that again shrouds me in sexual sadness. I have elected, after years of struggle, to remain faithful now to George; but even if I had not, I am aware that men no longer look at me "that way." This might well be so even if I weren't crippled, since a woman in her fifties does not arouse most men to passion, but my wheelchair seals my chastity. Men may look at me with pity, with affection, with amusement, with admiration, but never with lust. To be truthful, I have so internalized the social proscription of libido in my kind that if a man did come on to me, I'd probably distrust him as at least a little peculiar in his erotic tastes.

Anyway, except for George, I no longer look at men "that way" either. Whatever complicated motives—and the urge to prove that I was still desirable even though disabled certainly lurked among them—drove me in my twenties and thirties into the arms of a series of men have long since lost their force. I still like sex, but only with George, who cannot give me intercourse. But on this of all days, the fifth anniversary of his last cancer surgery, when against all odds he is not merely alive but well, when he will soon return from a full day's work and take me out for a celebratory dinner, I am mindful that sorrow, sexual or otherwise, does not necessarily bleed away life's sweetness. In fact, the consequences of George's impotence have been surprisingly mixed, since in precluding intercourse it has forced us to discover alternative means to intimacy.

Oddly and ironically, my disability provides one of these. I've heard it said that a sexual relationship cannot be sustained when one partner provides routine care to the disabled other. Perhaps so, if the relationship depends heavily on glamour, as I suppose a good many do. After thirty-five years of acquaintance, and with two catastrophic illnesses, if we demanded enchantment, we'd be sorely let down. Our bodies hold few mysteries for each other. Once you've helped your wife change her wet pants, or watched the surgeon pop a colony of E. coli from the healing wound in your husband's belly, you have seen behind all the veils. I don't know what the sexual bond between us relies on, but it's not sorcery. The routine of caregiving doesn't seem to diminish our attraction; George's impotence, which has a physiological rather than a psychological basis, doesn't usually discourage either of us from lovemaking. And because we have grown so familiar with each other's physical realities, we love each other more unabashedly and inventively as time goes on.

Whether for making love or not, our bodies—one twisted and nearly inert, the other scarified, both softening now with age and indulgence—instinctively seek each other out. Even our most mundane interactions bear an erotic charge. I don't mean that we pant and grope every time he tugs my sweater over my head or adjusts my bedclothes. Rutting adolescence lies many years in our wake. But he may stroke my neck when he brings me a cup of coffee. And since my wheelchair places me just at the height of his penis (though *Cock-High in the World* struck me as just too indecorous a book title), I may nuzzle it in return. We carry on a constant, often hardly conscious, corporeal conversation regardless of our other pursuits and preoccupations. Without my disability to throw us together thus habitually, our bodies might spend their days racing separately from one activity to another, coming across each other only in time to tumble into sleep.

The panic George's illness arouses in me stems in part from dread of the day when, without his steady and tender regard, I will have to keep my self going. Increasingly, as a body, I am turning into a set of problems: a bulk to be raised from the bed and maneuvered from one location to another; long, awkward arms and legs to be thrust into sleeves and pantlegs, stockings, shoes; a stomach to be filled time and time again; hair and teeth to be kept clean and nails to be pared; bladder and kidneys to be kept free from infection; buttocks to be monitored for signs of decubiti. Made not just of flesh and blood but of metal and rubber, I must be loaded into the van, tied down, seatbelt fastened in order to be transported anywhere, then unfastened, untied, unloaded at my destination. The absence of curb cuts, the presence of even one step, too narrow a door—all present obstacles.

No one but George, I fear, has reason to see me as more than the sum of my problems. Without him I would feel reduced to my nuisance value. I am terrified, against all reason, of being abused in retaliation. No one has ever, except by accident, hurt me. Matthew himself recalls most poignantly "The Day I Knocked Mom Down": "We were all arguing around the dining room table, raised voices, red faces, the whole deal. Hell, I can't even remember what we were going on about, something to do with my latest badness I suppose, but at any rate, fuses were short and I was leaving the realm of rational thought. Then my mother, innocently enough, tried to leave the table; god knows what I was thinking or why it was so important to finish my point, but I did try to shove her back into her chair. And those next few seconds will certainly follow me forever. The look of shock on her face as she collapsed, missing the chair entirely, the pure anger emanating from my dad (angriest I've ever seen him), the knowledge that I really had to go now and that something had changed forever and that there would be no returning from this event, these are the impressions that remain of that moment."

He can't have been more than sixteen, a hot-headed clumsy adolescent, and I would give anything to eradicate this mischance from his memory. Too much time has passed for it to serve us. For a while it made me wary of him, true, in the way that I was nervous about driving after a car bashed the rear end of my Kharmann Ghia when I braked at a yellow light in 1964. I drove for twenty-five more years, though. I go on mothering Matthew with the same ease.

He does not pose the threat I feel. Instead, I have visions of enduring life at the hands of strangers: refused food or drink, shoved roughly into bed, allowed to slip from my wheelchair and abandoned in a puddle of my own urine. These horrors, arising naturally, if irrationally, from physical helplessness, reflect an utter lack of self-regard. This is not what George has taught me. If I don't want to be reduced to a constellation of problems, I must imagine my body as something other than problematic: a vehicle for enmeshing the life I have been given into the lives of others. Easy enough to say. But to do? Who will have me? And on what terms?

In biblical times, physical and mental disorders were thought to signify possession by demons. In fact, Jesus's proficiency at casting these out accounted for much of his popularity among the common folk (though probably not among swine). People who were stooped or blind or subject to seizures were clearly not okay as they were but required fixing, and divine intervention was the only remedy powerful enough to cleanse them of their baleful residents.

Theologically as well as medically, this interpretation of the body in trouble now seems primitive, and yet we perpetuate the association underlying it. A brief examination of "dead" metaphors (those which have been so thoroughly integrated into language that we generally overlook their analogical origins) demonstrates the extent to which physical vigor equates with positive moral qualities. "Keep your chin up," we say (signifying courage), "and your eyes open" (alertness); "stand on your own two feet" (independence) "and tall" (pride); "look straight in the eye" (honesty) or "see eye to eye" (accord); "run rings around" (superiority). By contrast, physical debility connotes vice, as in "sit on your ass" (laziness), "take it lying down" (weakness), "listen with half an ear" (inattention), and get left "without a leg to stand on" (unsound argument). The way in which the body occupies space and the quality of the space it occupies correlate with the condition of the soul: it is better to be admired as "high-minded" than "looked down on" for one's "low morals," to be "in the know" than "out of it," to be "up front" than "back-handed," to be "free as a bird" than "confined to a wheelchair."

Now, the truth is that, unless you are squatting or six years old, I can never look you straight in the eye, and I spend all my time sitting on my ass except when I'm taking it lying down. These are the realities of life in a wheelchair (though in view of the alternatives—bed, chair, or floor—"confinement" is the very opposite of my condition). And the fact that the soundness of the body so often serves as a metaphor for its moral health, its deterioration thus implying moral degeneracy, puts me and my kind in a quandary. How can I possibly be "good"? Let's face it, wicked witches are not just ugly (as sin); they're also bent and misshapen (crooked). I am bent and misshapen, therefore ugly, therefore wicked. And I have no way to atone.

It is a bind many women, not just the ones with disabilities, have historically found themselves in by virtue of their incarnation in a sociolinguistic system over which they have had relatively little power. (Notice how virile the virtues encoded in the examples above.) Female bodies, even handsome and wholesome ones, have tended to give moralists fits of one sort or another (lust, disgust, but seldom trust). As everyone who has read the *Malleus Maleficarum* knows, "All witchcraft comes from carnal Lust which is in Women insatiable." If a good man is hard to find, a good woman is harder, unless she's (1) prepubescent, (2) senile, or (3) dead; and even then, some will have their doubts about her. It is tricky enough, then, trying to be a good woman at all, but a crippled woman experiences a kind of double jeopardy. How can she construct a world that will accommodate her realities, including her experience of her own goodness, while it remains comprehensible to those whose world-views are founded on premises alien or even inimical to her sense of self?

Disability is at once a metaphorical and a material state, evocative of other conditions in time and space— childhood and imprisonment come to mind—yet "like" nothing but itself. I can't live it or write about it except by conflating the figurative and the substantial, the "as if" with the relentlessly "what is." Let me illustrate with an experience from a couple of years ago, when George and I went to a luncheon honoring the Dalai Lama, held at a large resort northwest of Tucson. Although we were not enrolled in the five-day workshop he had come here to lead, we found ourselves in the hallway when the meeting room disgorged the workshop participants—all fourteen hundred of them—into a narrow area further constricted by tables laden with bells, beads, and brochures. And let me tell you, no matter how persuaded they were of the beauty and sacredness of all life, not one of them seemed to think that any life was going on below the level of her or his own gaze. "Down here!" I kept whimpering at the hips and buttocks and bellies pressing my wheelchair on all sides. "Down here! There's a person down here!" My only recourse was to roll to one side and hug a wall.

Postmodern criticism, feminist and otherwise, makes a good deal of the concept of wall-hugging, or marginality, which is meant to suggest that some segment of the population—black, brown, yellow, or red, poor, female, lesbian, what have you—is shouldered to the side, heedlessly or not, by some perhaps more numerous and certainly more powerful segment, most frequently wealthy, well-educated Euro-American males. Regardless of the way marginality is conceived, it is never taken to mean that those on the margin occupy a physical space literally outside the field of vision of those in the center, so that the latter trip unawares and fall into the laps of those they have banished from consciousness unless these scoot safely out of the way. "Marginality" thus means something altogether different to me from what it means to social theorists. It is no metaphor for the power relations between one group of human beings and another but a literal description of where I stand (figuratively speaking): over here, on the edge, out of bounds, beneath your notice. I embody the metaphors. Only whether or not I like doing so is immaterial.

It may be this radical materiality of my circumstances, together with the sense I mentioned earlier that
defect and deformity bar me from the ranks of
"good" women, which have spurred me in the past, as
they no doubt will go on doing, to put the body at the
center of all my meditations, my "corpus," if you will.
Not that I always write *about* the body, though I often
do, but that I always write, consciously, *as* a body. (This
quality more than any other, I think, exiles my work
from conventional academic discourse. The guys may
be writing with the pen/penis, but they pretend at all
times to keep it in their pants.) And it is this—my—
crippled female body that my work struggles to redeem
through that most figurative of human tools: language.
Because language substitutes a no-thing for a thing,
whereas a body is pure thing through and through, this
task must fail. But inevitable disappointment does not
deprive labor of its authenticity.

And so I use inscription to insert my embodied self
into a world with which, over time, I have less and less
in common. Part of my effort entails reshaping both
that self and that world in order to reconcile the two. We
bear certain responsibilities toward each other, the
world and I, and I must neither remove myself from it
nor permit it to exclude me if we are to carry these out.
I can't become a "hopeless cripple" without risking
moral paralysis; nor can the world, except to its own di-
minishment, refuse my moral participation.

But is a woman for whom any action at all is nearly
impossible capable of right action, or am I just being
morally cocky here? After all, if I claim to be a good

woman, I leave myself open to the question: Good for what? The most straightforward answer is the most tempting: Good for nothing. I mean really. I can stand with assistance but I can't take a step; I can't even spread my own legs for sex anymore. My left arm doesn't work at all, and my right one grows weaker almost by the day. I am having more and more trouble raising a fork or a cup to my lips. (It is possible, I've discovered, though decidedly odd, to drink even coffee and beer through a straw.) I can no longer drive. I lack the stamina to go out to work. If I live to see them, I will never hold my own grandchildren. These incapacities constitute a stigma that, according to social scientist Erving Goffman, removes me from normal life into a "discredited" position in relation to society.[1]

From the point of view of the Catholic Church, to which I belong, however, mine must be just about the ideal state: too helpless even for the sins other flesh is heir to. After all, parties aren't much fun now that I meet the other revelers eye to navel, and getting drunk is risky since I can hardly see straight cold sober. No matter how insatiable my carnal Lust, nobody's likely to succumb to my charms and sully my reputation. But I am, by sympathy at least, a Catholic *Worker*, part of a community that wastes precious little time fretting about the seven deadlies, assuming instead that the moral core of being in the world lies in the care of others, in *doing* rather than *being* good. How can a woman identify herself as a Catholic Worker if she can't even cut up carrots for the soup or ladle it out for the hungry people queued up outside the kitchen door? Physical incapacity certainly appears to rob such a woman of moral efficacy.

Well, maybe moral demands should no longer be placed on her. Perhaps she ought simply to be "excused" from the moral life on the most generous of grounds: that she suffers enough already, that she has plenty to do just to take care of herself. This dismissive attitude tends to be reinforced when the woman lives at the height of your waist. Because she "stands" no higher than a six-year-old, you may unconsciously ascribe to her the moral development of a child (which, in view of Robert Coles's findings, you will probably underestimate) and demand little of her beyond obedience and enough self-restraint so that she doesn't filch candy bars at the checkout counter while you're busy writing a check. (God, I can't tell you how tempting those brightly wrapped chunks are when they're smack up against your nose.) "Stature" is an intrinsic attribute of moral life, and the woman who lacks the one may be judged incapable of the other.

I am exaggerating here, of course, but only a little. Beyond cheerfulness and patience, people don't generally expect much of a cripple's character. And certainly they presume that care, which I have placed at the heart of moral experience, flows in one direction, "downward": as from adult to child, so from well to ill, from whole to maimed. This condescension contributes to what Goffman calls "spoiled identity," though he does not deal satisfactorily with the damage it inflicts: without reciprocity, the foundation of any mature moral relationship, the person with a defect cannot grow "up" and move "out" into the world but remains constricted in ways that make being "confined to a wheelchair" look trivial. And so I would say that while it is all right to excuse me from making the soup (for the sake of the soup, probably more than "all right"), you must never—even with the best intentions, even with my own complicity—either enable or require me to withdraw from moral life altogether.

So much for carrot-cutting, then, or any other act involving sharp instruments. But wait! One sharp instrument is left me: my tongue. (Here's where metaphor comes in handy.) And my computer keyboard is . . . just waist high. With these I ought to be able to concoct another order of soup altogether (in which I'll no doubt find myself up to my ears). In other words, what I can still *do*—so far—is write books. Catholic Workers being extraordinarily tolerant of multiplicity, on the theory that it takes all kinds of parts to form a body, this activity will probably be counted good enough.

The world to which I am a material witness is a difficult one to love. But I am not alone in it now; and as the population ages, more and more people—a significant majority of them women—may join me in it, learning to negotiate a chill and rubble-strewn landscape with impaired eyesight and hearing and mobility, searching out some kind of home there. Maps render foreign territory, however dark and wide, fathomable. I mean to make a map. My infinitely harder task, then, is to conceptualize not merely a habitable body but a habitable world: a world that wants me in it.

Taking Care

THIS MORNING we've had a breakdown in the Nancy-care apparatus. On a new school schedule, George now has to get me up and dressed at 7:15, an arrangement that—since I'm neither an early nor a gracious riser—suits us badly. Recently, I've hired my sister, who has moved to the town just south of Tucson, to come on Wednesday mornings. This way, I can sleep till 8:00 or so at least one day a week, and then Sally can help me shower and dress, sort out the paperwork that accumulates in drifts throughout the house and studio, and then get us some lunch before returning to Green Valley in time for an afternoon swim while I settle down to write (or not write, at which I seem more proficient). This week, however, Mother has invited her to the Elks Ladies' Auxiliary luncheon, so we've arranged that she will come on Thursday instead.

I wake Wednesday morning restlessly, surfacing and

drifting and sinking and surfacing again as I wait for George to rush in, rouse and raise me, make the bed while I use the toilet, tug on my clothes, and give me a hasty kiss before dashing out of the house. It's bad enough having to get up at 7:15, and I'm irritated with myself for having awakened early. Finally I'm alert enough to peer at my watch. 8:20. Something must be wrong with George! (This leap is the legacy of the years we have lived with cancer.) But no. George must simply have forgotten that Sally's not coming till tomorrow. Or did I forget to tell him?

Well, no matter how I got this way, I am in a pickle. No one is coming to my rescue, not until George returns at 4:30 anyway, and not knowing that I was going to be alone, I haven't brought the portable telephone to bed with me, so I can't call for help. My bladder is full, and although I have kept a flannel-covered rubber sheet printed with gamboling blue lambs on my mattress for years, I have no desire to christen it. I reach for the control to my electric bed, lower my feet, and raise my head as far as it will go. The next part is tricky, since I have to work my legs over the edge and then push my trunk upright. A false move will pitch me onto my back like a beetle or forward into a heap on the floor; in either case, I'll be there for eight hours. Done! I've parked my wheelchair farther back than I would have if I had known I would have to fetch it on my own, but my fingertips just reach the controls and the chair glides forward. Can I shift my ass from mattress to cushion? Yes! I make it to the toilet only slightly damp.

As I drink the glass of apple juice George has left for

me in the refrigerator, I begin to formulate a bold plan. I have long wanted to see whether I still could manage on my own, and to what extent, but none of my family have been willing to let me. Here is a fortuitous occasion to test my capabilities without giving anybody fits. I decide I will not merely put on my own clothes but take a shower first.

Not an adventure on a grand scale, I'll admit, but for me it will require the concentration of walking a tightrope without a net. The myriad small actions that most people would perform all but unconsciously tax my ingenuity: removing the plastic wrist splint I wear to bed, unfastening my watch, pulling my nightgown over my head. Discovering that my towel is too heavy to get off its hook, I have to get back into my wheelchair and roll out to the linen closet for another. Then I have to figure out how to spread it out flat in the chair. I remember motions I haven't performed in years—the way one grasps the edges of a towel and snaps it flat and drapes it—while slowly and awkwardly inventing new motions to replace them.

Finally I'm ready for the shower itself. I leave the water cold, even though I hate the sensation, because I know how heat aggravates MS symptoms. Even so, getting out is the scariest part of the operation, the tile floor slippery under my wet feet, creating a vertiginous instant between letting go of one grab bar and grasping another. Praying as I plunk, I land in the wheelchair. With the towel under me to protect the cushions, I can't rub myself dry. I should have brought two towels.

Live and learn. Fortunately, it's September, still hot in Tucson, and the air will do the job. A dab of deodorant. A spritz of cologne. Unders, loose shorts, a T-shirt, sandals. A few minutes in front of the mirror with makeup and comb, and I'm as presentable as I'm going to get.

One more project: something to eat. Generally George sets out a salad or a bowl of fruit in the refrigerator for me but today, of course, he believes Sally's in charge. A couple of restaurants are close enough to get to, but rolling there will consume more time and energy than I can spare. Better explore the refrigerator. Hmm. George must have had a bad morning, because he has forgotten not just me but his lunch: a peanut butter sandwich and some brownish substance in a plastic container which I don't care to contemplate. Eventually I come up with part of a container of cottage cheese and half a red pear, which I promptly drop cut side down and have to hold under the faucet, hoping the dog and cat hairs wash away. These trophies, together with the few crackers left in an open packet, will do me nicely.

The two-liter bottle of Coke is nearly full, wouldn't you know. I put my mug in the sink and pull myself to my feet in front of it. The view from the high window looks odd to me, and I realize that since I stood here last, before I gave up cooking five years ago, more of the privet has died and been cleared away, baring the white brick wall of the house next door. With both hands, I tip the bottle, pouring a good bit of Coke down the sink but more into the mug. Afraid of more spills if I try to move everything into the dining room, I picnic at the pullout cutting board.

And now here I am in front of the computer, limp but victorious: clean, clothed, and fed. I can hardly wait for George to get home so I can gloat. He'll be horrified, I know, but also hopeful at this sign that I'm not yet wholly incapacitated. We both recognize that such efforts aren't a wise use of my limited resources and that the more often I tried to repeat them, no matter how cautiously, the more likely some serious mishap would become. I owe much of today's triumph to pure luck. We both know—the unmade bed, the crumpled damp towel, the dirty dishes all attest—that left entirely to my own devices, I would soon founder in messes of my own making. We both understand that, over time, my competence at even the simplest tasks will decrease rather than increase. But for this moment we can bask in a brief respite from dread.

The human infant must be hardwired to utter the phrase "I can do it myself" at about the age of two, so insistent is the drive toward self-care. By this time, she has achieved a physically independent stance, as Judith Viorst describes in *Necessary Losses*:

> Practice makes perfect, crawling yields to walking, and at this momentous point in the practicing stage, upright locomotion permits such vistas, such possibilities, such triumphs, that a child can grow drunk on omnipotence and grandeur. We turn into flaming narcissists. And megalomaniacs. The masters of all

we survey. The view from the top of two moving legs has seduced us into a love affair with the world. It, and we, are wonderful.[1]

In this heady state, the child lives in a maelstrom of scattered Cheerios, mismatched socks and knotted shoelaces, snarly hair, spilled juice, and wet training pants. After what may seem to a beleaguered parent to be an eternity but is really an astonishingly short span, however, she has mastered spoons and napkins and combs and even her bladder, so that by the time she goes off to school, she really can do almost everything herself. Before long, she has forgotten both her infantile helplessness and her struggle for competence, but their vestiges lodge permanently in her unconscious. With luck, nothing will ever rouse them, and she will sail confidently through the rest of her life.

I didn't have such luck. That's how I know about those traces of old dependencies: the same furious frustration that fuels a two-year-old's temper tantrums often grips me, as my body reverts toward its infantile state. The difference is that whereas such emotion stimulated the two-year-old's progress, it merely tears me apart, since I will never again grow drunk on the world viewed from atop two moving legs, and "I can do it myself" is less and less a statement of fact or of possibility than of unmeetable desire. No longer can I count on practice making perfect, as I could in childhood. Effort and will have lost their meaning. But the craving for personal independence remains as alive and well as it was fifty years ago when my mother, hugely pregnant, had to put a harness on me so that I couldn't out-run her. Myelin dissolves, nerves short out, muscle at-rophies, but the old brain, riddled now with sclerotic patches, goes on wailing, "I can do it myself!"

To complicate matters, I am addicted to solitude and silence, so that I wish to accomplish tasks not merely myself but *by* myself. My most contented memories, at least from early adolescence onward, are unpopu-lated—solitary hours of reading, tramping, cycling—or peopled only by strangers on trains, subways, buses, in the city when I was old enough to venture off on my own. The habit of retreat is so thoroughly entrenched now that unless I can spend several hours of every day in seclusion, my nerves soon begin to feel like catgut scraped by an unrosined bow.

For us who cannot always take care of ourselves (and of whom is that not true?) there is an etiquette to taking care from others, which demands a considerable degree of the very sociability that I lack. True, some people with disabilities persist in willful and often vociferous independence, manners be damned. In *Moving Viola-tions*, John Hockenberry relates his characteristic re-sponse "when people wanted to push my chair, or hold a door, or hand me something they thought I was look-ing at on a supermarket shelf. With a workable, relaxed face of self-assured confidence I could dismiss all of these people politely or rudely, but dismiss them I did. 'No need to be concerned,' I said. 'I've got the door. I am fine. I can make it across the street. No problem. I'm not sick. I don't need a push. I'm not with anyone, no.' "[2] I suppose that this dismissiveness feels appropriate, even necessary, for someone who conveys a sense that social interaction is a rather joyless game: "I could go away or push ahead," Hockenberry writes of his intrusion into others' space. "Going away was always a defeat. Pushing ahead was never a victory, and asking for help always reduced the score."

By contrast, I view my crippled life less as a contest than as a project, in which others must participate if it is to prosper. Because I use what Hockenberry scorns as a "wimp" chair, with arm rests, batteries, foam-filled tires, and brakes that lock automatically when I release the joystick, no one can propel me but me (though they do instinctively try, and I'll confess a secret amusement at their thwarted efforts). But I can't open weighted doors, reach high shelves, lift anything heavier than a paperback book, even write out my own checks, and I enlist aid right and left. I also usually accept it even when I haven't solicited it, because being brushed off, even politely, can hurt people's feelings, and then they become wary of cripples in general.

Sometimes the attention can be offensive, God knows. Hockenberry recounts a horrific encounter with a flight attendant:

"I guess you are the first handicapped person I have ever seen up close. Have you ever thought of killing yourself?"

I wondered if this question appeared in this flight attendant's official training manual under the heading of "Handicapped Patrons: Suggested Conversation Starters."

"Do you ask lots of people on your airline if they think of suicide?"

"Oh, goodness no, that would be crazy. I was just wondering about you because you get around so well that you must have really done a lot of praying to get this great attitude."

My great attitude was eroding fast.[3]

I have never had a conversation quite this outrageous—or if I have, I've forgotten it—but I routinely encounter familiarity I find inappropriate, and I try to accept it as though the person were merely a curious two-year-old to my furious one. One of us just has to grow up. I don't think it's the normals' own fault that they lack disabilities to deepen and complicate their understanding of the world. Mine is alien terrain, and strangers are bound to make gaffes in it.

Visiting Zaïre some years ago, I learned that a woman may, and often does, bare her breasts, but thighs carry the same erotic charge that breasts do in the States and are always covered by two pagnes, lengths of brightly colored cloth wrapped and secured with a deft twist at the waist. The Zaïroises we met were unfailingly polite and would probably have looked the other way if I'd hiked my skirt up getting into and out of the car; but I was glad to have my daughter, who lived there, to save me from this particular solecism. I guess I think of myself, like Anne, as a cultural mediary. Some of the tourists in my country can be gauche, but if I instruct them patiently, maybe they'll absorb some of the mores and feel at ease.

But the didactic role can get tiresome, and I'm always relieved when I encounter someone who already knows—through experience or empathy—what I need without direction and provides it all but invisibly. Part of the reason I prefer George's assistance—indeed, part of the reason that I fell in love with him in the first place—may be that he makes me feel more alone than anyone else I know. I don't mean lonely, although there have been periods in our thirty-five years of acquaintance when he has left me bitterly lonely as well. I mean simply that he doesn't expect a social performance. He would, of course, prefer me to be civil, as I am not always, but his criteria for civility aren't severe—pretty much anything short of a snarl will pass. And he never expects to be entertained, instructed, exhorted, or uplifted, although I flatter myself that I provide all these services in some measure. He just expects me to be there.

Moreover, after so many years together, we tend to communicate telegraphically. Not that we don't engage in full, lengthy, and impassioned discussion. But at the mundane level, where most of my needs for assistance reside, we carry out tasks almost without comment. The other night, for instance, at a family birthday party at my parents' house, I became so engaged in general conversation that I forgot to monitor my bladder, as I often do in company, until catastrophe threatened.

"George?" I said softly across the room.

"Toilet?" he responded, rising quickly, and we trundled down the hallway to the bathroom, which, because it lacks grab bars, I can't use alone.

"Whew!" I said gratefully as he yanked down my trousers and lowered me. "That was close!"

"You did look . . . distressed," he laughed. No doubt. His knowing what that look signified, however—not that my shoes were too tight or that I'd chomped down on a piece of hard candy and broken a tooth or that I'd suddenly remembered some long-repressed traumatic event from my childhood—probably saved me by seconds from A Very Bad Accident.

This almost intuitive communication, which can evolve between people who live in intimacy and affection over a long span, offers inexpressible comfort, and in our precarious circumstances, both of us want comforting more than most. He tells me he is no more eager to relinquish his caregiving role—which he finds "seductive, because the world esteems me for it"—than I am to hire outside assistance.

Nevertheless, we both know that as my condition deteriorates, he can't take on the extra work without growing weary and grumpy. "Nancy is outspoken about her wants," he reflects, "and if they are not met, she will complain . . . as why shouldn't she? Her incontinence pad is crooked. Her frigid chicken dinner is still frigid. The toilet paper I've bought for her toilet is cheap and scratchy. And her pillow needs adjusting before I can get into bed and turn out the light. I try to imagine what it would be like to have so little control over such simple, everyday circumstances. I can't. Again and again I suffer either aloud or to myself: Who do I complain to? Who will straighten my pillow? What would it be like to be able to say, 'It's her fault that the ironing didn't get done'? What would it be like to have no one—especially me—say that the bed didn't get made because George didn't get it done?"

He must have respite. Already we have a housekeeper six hours a week and Sally another five. Sally provides an ideal transition between George's care and that of a professional home health aide because, having known her since she was three weeks old and my grandmother returned me to my newly and shockingly expanded household, I feel closer to her than to anyone except George. I hope she'll find a "real" job, though; and even if she doesn't, she has a home of her own to tend.

Adrienne Asch, an expert in disability issues, divorces the word "care" from "assistance" or "help," in fact, and suggests that "assistance with activities of daily living . . . might best be provided by people who are *not* family members" because there is "no necessary connection between loving a parent, sibling, or spouse and providing such help."[4] Although I feel personally untroubled by using "care" to cover both situations, and although our arrangements suit George and me for the moment, her point is well taken. No affection, only a steady hand, is required for shaving my underarms; and no one who loves me should feel thereby obliged to tie my boots. But how will we ever pay for the amount of assistance I am likely to need in the future?

Such dilemmas haunt thousands upon thousands of others throughout the country, many less fortunate than I in terms of family support, and the numbers will only grow as longevity extends and the population ages. The dread of being a burden—emotional, physical, financial—on those one loves can only be inflamed by lawmakers with fat wallets and excellent health insurance who feel free to slash medical care for the elderly and people with disabilities in order to reward—guess who?—people with fat wallets and excellent health insurance. (A professed Christian, I am ashamed to own the distinctly ungenerous wish that each one of them, sleek and smug, would be stricken with multiple sclerosis.) Such measures reflect the attitude that those of us who require care constitute an intolerable burden upon society, that we have nothing to offer to the human project, that we are, in fact, not worth taking care of. This implication breaks my heart. I am reduced to a vortex, sucking in the resources of all around me without replenishing them in kind.

Although I never much wanted to become a nurse, as little girls often do, many of my childhood fantasies involved rescuing and ministering to a loved one who was injured or ill. What a thrill of gratification they gave me! And I still remember my pride when Aunt Elsie, my grandfather's sister, came to call and I made her a cup of tea. Heaven knows why I was at home alone.

Mother must have run out on a quick errand. At any rate, I was determined to treat Aunt Elsie, a rotund and cheerful widow, with the courtesy I knew grownups lavished on one another, although—equally gracious— she protested that I needn't put myself out. I wasn't allowed to use the stove, I told her, and so I drenched her teabag in tap water as hot as I could run it. Mother soon returned to find Aunt Elsie valiantly sipping away at the tepid brew, all compliments for my excellent services, though glad enough to accept a fresh cup made with boiling water. I basked in my sense of accomplishment.

Now look at me: utterly useless. Sitting on what my mother used to call my "dead duff." When someone comes to the house, I can point out the kettle, the teabags, the cups, but she will have to make her own tea. Which of course she'll be glad to do. But that's not the point. The point is that even trivial service satisfies a longing. Deprived of the means to perform it, I feel wasted and empty.

You would think, then, that I would admit at least the possibility of the same need in others, but I seldom do. During George's gravest illness a few years ago, my daughter accompanied me to my neurologist for a routine checkup. My condition was clearly deteriorating, and I was panicky. "I just don't know what will become of me when George dies," I said.

"What about your children?" Dr. Johnson asked, glancing at Anne's small form in the corner of the examining room. "Won't they take care of you?"

"No," I said quickly, proudly, firmly. "That's not who I want to be in their lives." I didn't recognize till long afterward the arrogance of my reply, the way in which it foreclosed their option to take me in and look after me, like it or not. It *isn't* who I want to be in their lives, and I don't suppose it's who they want me to be in their lives, either. But instead of speaking, I should at least have turned to Anne with a questioning look and seen what she had to say. Perhaps, even though I'm not exactly the woman any of us wants me to be, my children want to—need to—take care of me.

Just recently, the letter of a friend who is widowed, blind, and in poor health crystallized this insight for me. She lamented her dependence on "the visiting nurse, the nurse's aide, the cleaning lady, not to mention my children who have to read me my mail, do my laundry, buy my groceries. I sometimes think I am being extremely selfish to try to stay on in my own home since it inconveniences so many people to have me do so. Leaving home is a sacrifice I'm not quite ready to make—although it might be good for my soul!" I replied that her children might well be finding her care good for their souls and that perhaps she owed them that opportunity. As usual, I talk a better story than I live.

I am not being flippant. I really do believe that actively nurturing your fellow creatures through serving them, in what the Catholic Church designates as the corporal works of mercy, develops and disciplines the whatever-you-call-it: the part of the human psyche that transcends self-interest. This may be why I feel comfortable using "care" as Adrienne Asch does not, because it has a wider significance for me than familial affection. I believe also that not performing these very literal works—feeding and clothing and sheltering—diminishes what I call the soul. I know that alms-giving fulfills my church-defined obligation in this regard, but duty isn't my chief concern. I yearn to act out my love, in the way that a dancer inscribes abstract movements on the air with hands and feet and torso and head in order to give her private vision public force. I want to *do* love.

In particular, I want to love my husband in this dynamic way, as he will need if the melanoma that has plagued him for a decade recurs. Five years ago, when abdominal surgery required him to spend ten days in hospital, I was already too damaged myself to be of much use, but at least I could stay on a cot in his room. Now, too weak to get up unassisted, I would have to remain at home with an aide. Even if he were at home, I couldn't smooth his pillow, empty basins and urinals, rub his back, fix him a tempting bite to eat—the kind of little gestures familiar to me from years of big-sistering and mothering—and the idleness would drive me nuts. Literally. I get very frightened when George is ill, and without physical activity to distract me, my interior life grows dim and distorted.

Nor can I serve in other situations. When my beloved aunt was laid up for weeks by the repair of an abdominal aneurysm, and later by pneumonia, I couldn't fly to her side as I longed to do. When my niece was felled by a stroke just as her parents were preparing to move across country, I couldn't go to her and her disabled husband, either. If my aging parents require assistance, I won't be the one to provide it. I'll never dandle a grandbaby on my knee. I can't even take Lucky Pup and the two geriatric cats to the vet for their shots. I haven't the strength to drive a truck loaded with school supplies to the campesinos in Nicaragua or even to scrub soup pots at Our Lady of Guadalupe Free Kitchen.

These incapacities are the source of a grief inconsolable and perhaps incomprehensible to anyone still rushing from one good deed to the next and wishing for a chance to put up her weary feet. My feet are up, on the plastic platform of my wheelchair, permanently. No one blames me, I know; and I don't feel guilty, because guilt depends on action—either the commission of a wrong one or the omission of a right one—and I *can't* act. Instead, I feel overwhelmingly wistful, beyond all hope of surcease. "But you take such wonderful care of me," George demurs when I confide my sorrow. "You make me feel so loved!" And then, after a moment: "I can understand what you're getting at, though. I think I'd feel the same way if I couldn't take care of you."

In his quiet affirmation lies all the comfort I'm going to get, and I'm grateful that he doesn't feel compelled to rush to my rescue in a flurry of denials and remonstrances. I can't be cajoled out of a regret so deep, though plenty of people, panicked in the face of such strong and baffling emotion, would try, more for their own comfort than for mine. The last thing I need are hearty protestations that what I can or cannot do doesn't really matter. Where is the consolation in those? Though meant to reassure me of my fundamental value, I suppose, they merely suggest to me that any potential contributions I might have made wouldn't have counted for much anyway and so the world misses me much less than I miss it. I prefer to think that the world lost a bit when I was knocked out of it, and that mourning is an inevitable and appropriate response to such a rupture.

If rage and sadness are left unacknowledged and unaccepted, they transmute readily into depression, to which I have always been susceptible. Better, I have learned, to open oneself wide to them, and then wider still, to permit them to sweep on through. They come in ceaseless waves, but each trough between them provides a tranquil moment in which to figure out how to act. My serious shortcomings in "taking care" in all senses of the phrase—exercising caution, accepting the ministrations of others, or offering aid and consolation—do not absolve me of responsibilities. I have to work out right behaviors with whatever skills are left to me.

I must be careful physically, for example, searching out the line between doing all that I safely can and taking silly risks. An injury as simple as a broken wrist, which would merely inconvenience most people, could incapacitate me completely, by preventing me from driving my wheelchair. Thus, regardless of the rush of satisfaction my morning of stolen independence has brought me, it held too many chancy moments to furnish a practical pattern for my day-to-day existence. True, I can take precautions, like carrying the portable telephone around with me, but the last thing I want is to play I've-Fallen-and-I-Can't-Get-Up with a bunch of paramedics while I'm soaked and stark naked and slippery on the shower floor. I must discipline myself, then, to turn my body over to strangers under conditions less offensive to my sensibilities. I don't have to like this. Nobody *has* to like anything. I just have to do it.

If I'm not going to make life wretched for myself and everyone assisting me, however, I'd better do it with some grace. I'm half a century beyond two years old now, after all. I may feel like having a temper tantrum, but in most cases I can't just act the impulse out. As for solitude, I may have to learn to get along with less of it, but I must also train myself to ask for it when necessary. Creeping off by myself always aroused at least a whiff of disapproval when I was growing up, and in company I was expected to hold up my end of a conversation whether I felt like talking or not. Fearful of appearing monstrously antisocial, I have never been able to say, "I need to be alone, or at least silent, for a while." Once I've mastered this line—and really it's not so dreadful, not half as complicated as a Shakespearean sonnet, nowhere near as rude as "your mother wears army boots"—I may relax into others' hands willingly enough.

Permitting myself to be taken care of is, in fact, one of the ways I can take care of others. This past summer, George's mother asked him to take her but not me to Vermont for a few days. When I mentioned to my mother that I thought I might try to manage on my own, she burst out: "You certainly will not! What if your house caught fire in the night? I'll come to stay with you." I protested, but only half-heartedly. For one thing, I had some serious doubts about my ability to keep myself and the pets fed. More important, I recognized that I was hardly freeing others by throwing them into a tizzy. George's trip would be spoiled if he spent the whole time imagining me in one scrape or another. As it was, he had to telephone three times in five days to make sure that Mother and I were managing. (We were, in fact, relishing some time together outside the noisy chaos of our usual large family gatherings.) For the most part, he got a well-deserved respite. An odd love offering—my absence rather than my presence— but one that, thanks to Mother, was within my power to make.

I have to improvise these alternatives to the traditional modes of tendering care, and I must learn to trust others to find them adequate. Since most physical acts are denied me, my efforts must take largely intellectual and emotional form. I've become a closer and more patient listener, and I spend time giving information, counsel, and encouragement, especially to people with cancer and MS, as well as to students and other fledgling writers. I also express appreciation and approval and affection much more readily: Once afraid of "gush-ing," I've turned into a positive freshet and to hell with Yankee reticence. Above all, I can still write, which for me has always been an act of oblation and nurturance: my means of taking the reader into my arms, holding a cup to her lips, stroking her forehead, whispering jokes into her ears. . . .

With such gestures, I am taking all the care I can.

THE WIDER WORLD

Opening Doors, Unlocking Hearts

THE WORLD as it is currently constructed does not especially want—and plainly does not need—me in it. That statement seems so destined to elicit a rush of reassurances (*oh my dear of course we want you you have so much to contribute and then so many people depend on you for love your children especially and you have so many friends*) that I need to stop a moment to let them play out before I go on to explain.

That done, I shall proceed. I don't mean to belittle reminders of my worth. I crave them just as much as every other human being does, and I employ a variety of devices to solicit them, some more honorable than others, but my opening sentence doesn't happen to be one of them. And I don't want its force undermined by denial and pity, no matter how lovingly intended. I mean simply that much of the time, as a disabled woman, I find that my physical and social environments send the message that my presence is not unequivocally either welcome or vital. I am not looking for reassurances just now. I want to change the world.

I'm not overly ambitious. I'm willing to start small. With your house, for instance. Suppose I came to call. (Don't start shoving dirty laundry into the closet. I'm not on my way. This is just a thought experiment.) To begin with, could I get onto the front porch to ring the doorbell? Probably not. I can't even get to my own, since there are several steps from the street and several more onto the porch itself. Fortunately, the single one from the back porch was easy enough to ramp; but now that the sliding glass door is getting too heavy for me, I'm having to contemplate installing an electric door. The trouble with a degenerative disease is that no accommodation is ever final.

Presumably, however, if I can get to it, you will open your door for me, and I will roll in. Front doors are generally wide enough for my wheelchair, which at about twenty-two inches is narrower than standard, but interior doors, especially in newish houses, often are not wide enough. Can I, for instance, fit into the bathroom? (Like many other people with MS, I have an unpredictable bladder, and if I'm going to make any but the briefest visit, I'll have to put the bathroom to the test.) But never mind. The toilet will be low, and without grab bars I won't be able to transfer on and off anyway. Just don't offer me any liquid refreshment.

Well, you get the idea. The space through which you move comfortably without a thought, skirting the coffee table there, slipping sideways behind that chair to reach for a novel on the fifth shelf of the bookcase, looms with obstacles for me. And although I do not expect you to reconstruct it to permit me access, a number of problems could have been eliminated in the initial design. Builders, installing towel bars anyway, could just as well make them grab bars; even world-class athletes can slip getting out of the shower. Grab bars are available that don't look like hospital fittings. Of course, the reason they are not installed routinely is cost, but if they were manufactured in sufficient numbers for the whole construction industry, the difference would be marginal.

Certainly contractors who see a market make modifications as a matter of course. In Green Valley, the retirement community south of Tucson where my parents live, houses are constructed with thirty-six-inch doorways, open floor plans and wide halls, and small details like rocking electric switches and elongated doorknobs. Since elderly people, however robust initially, may need walkers or wheelchairs at some point and aren't going to want to undertake major remodeling when they do, the adaptations are built in from the outset. And although the prices strike me as exorbitant, they aren't above average for my part of the country.

What ultimately prohibits such construction from being standard is not cost but obliviousness fed, without doubt, by denial. *Oh no,* says the young couple buying their first home, *we don't have to think about such terrible things, nothing bad is going to happen to our bodies, not for years and years and years.* (I know. I was twenty-five when we bought our first house, a duplex that required us to climb a couple of long flights of stairs several times every day. By chance, we had only just sold it and moved to Arizona when I got my diagnosis.) I'm not arguing that vigorous people of any age ought to fret about contracting chronic incurable degenerative diseases or spinal-cord injuries or even the normal ills and ails of advancing age. On the contrary, I'm saying that if they can buy thoughtfully constructed houses, they will have one less reason to worry about such prospects.

Of course, these are not changes that can be mandated except by demand. The design and furnishing of private homes is almost entirely a matter of personal taste molded by current fashion, and builders and interior decorators will do just about anything to a space that they believe will help it sell. As the baby boomers gray, living to unprecedented ages, I may find more and more of their homes accessible, even commodious. In the meantime, we can always meet at a restaurant.

Or can we? When it comes to public spaces, some of the conditions and issues are rather different. Without explicit invitation, I have no right to enter your home, which has, by long-standing tradition, been assigned a figurative moat (yard), drawbridge (porch), and portcullis (bolted door) in case I forget myself. But I ought to be admitted to any place to which the general populace commonly has access: restaurants, surely, as well as banks, churches, theaters and cinemas, the post office, dry-cleaning shops, beauty salons, and above all the mall! You'd think that a capitalist society would eagerly grasp this principle without legal intervention: the more goods and services I can readily reach, the more likely I am to spend my money. In reality, legislation has often been required to ensure access, which has been slow to be established and is still far from perfect. The Americans with Disabilities Act (ADA) of 1990, federally mandating equal opportunity for people with physical and mental impairments, has only begun to have some discernible effects.

If I'm to make my contribution to capitalism, of course, I must have some money of my own to spend. According to one magazine article, "a staggering 67 percent of the 43 million Americans with disabilities are unemployed, and 82 percent of those individuals want to work"[1] rather than live on the dole. Employment was one of the major issues ADA was designed to address. It requires employers to hire qualified personnel without regard to disability and to make modifications, as long as these do not impose "undue hardship," to accommodate their special needs. Employers balk mechanically at mandates, as a friend from high school who owns his own business made clear one evening, claiming that such a law threatened to bankrupt him. He didn't even fall under its provisions, I had to point out to him, since he had fewer than the twenty-five employees originally required for it to take force or even the fifteen to which the limit has now been lowered; and the "undue hardship" clause protects businesses from unreasonable levels of expense. Moreover, many modifications—a ramp to a door, say—don't cost a great deal but, if done properly, last virtually forever, so that my friend himself, should he suffer a stroke years hence, might benefit from work done now.

In return for a relatively modest outlay, an employer is likely to get an exceptional worker. People with disabilities, like other disadvantaged groups, know that they are scrutinized relentlessly for shortcomings and expected to fail. Work of average quality won't gain them the necessary edge over fellow workers they are required (in all kinds of subtle, perhaps even subconscious ways, by themselves as well as by others) to show in order to earn a place among "normals." You may consider yourself entitled by education and experience to a particular job. I consider myself entitled by education and experience to such a job *even though I'm a cripple*. The qualifier is inescapable. As a consequence, a disabled person is likely to suffer from Supercrip Syndrome, which may half-kill her but affords an employer the benefits of diligence, low absenteeism, and long-term commitment.

Despite its guarantee of equal opportunity for disabled workers, however, ADA hasn't yet succeeded in raising levels of employment. Employers who continue to drag their feet contribute, probably quite heavily, to the problem. To change attitudes among the disabled presents a challenge as well. Some, of course, are simply too impaired, ill, or aged to be employable no matter how well adapted the workplace becomes. Others, who depend on Social Security for income and medical care, find themselves penalized for working, principally because they lose Medicare or Medicaid coverage without being guaranteed any other health insurance. More subtly but more perniciously, raised in a society that equates "disability" with "sickness" and "helplessness," more than a few, especially among the congenitally disabled, simply cannot envision any productive roles for themselves. Only with a new model, which defines people with disabilities very precisely in terms not of what they cannot (any longer) do but of what they can, will the world stop imposing this unwholesome sort of dependency.

Getting a job is one thing; getting *to* it is another. Not everyone can run out the door, a coat in one hand and a piece of toast in the other, jump onto a bicycle or into a car, and join the morning rush to the office. Many disabled people do drive, perhaps using adaptations like wheelchair lifts and hand controls, but plenty do not, and the lack of public transportation often constricts a life more sharply than any disability does. When my mother-in-law's macular degeneration progressed to the point that she could no longer see the road, for instance, she reluctantly left the small Vermont town she loved and moved to a retirement complex in Tucson, where a van is available for the trips to the market and the doctor she was accustomed to making on her own.

Independent travel is easier in cities operating public buses now that ADA requires all new vehicles to be wheelchair-accessible. In Tucson, the fixed-route system is augmented by Van Tran, which operates a large fleet of minibuses providing door-to-door service for only $1.20 each way (less for people with low incomes). Since one must reserve a ride at least a day in advance, often dialing for an hour or more before reaching an operator, the system allows for no spontaneity; but it frees hundreds of users a day to attend the local community college or university, travel to and from work, visit doctors, see a film or a play, or simply hang out at the mall for a couple of hours.[2]

All these public venues must be accessible, according to ADA. As with private residences, it is easier to design and build a new structure than to modify an old one. I'm lucky that I chanced to move from Boston, with its high-curbed, crooked, cobbled streets and historic buildings looming above long flights of granite steps and its ubiquitous double sets of doors to keep the bluster at bay, to a flat and open region, much of which still resembles a vast construction site. Alas, even in Tucson, architects do not appear to have been taught that the spaces they fantasize so extravagantly will one day be occupied by human beings of any stripe, and so the newness of a building does not guarantee its user-friendliness. I'd like to see every architecture and construction firm required to retain a disabled consultant, preferably one in a wheelchair, who would evaluate every structure as it was being planned and erected for the ease with which people can move through it.

The area that would get my closest scrutiny would be the rest rooms, which ought to be something of a national scandal. The general belief appears to be that if you provide one stall with a wide opening, a raised toilet, and a bar on the wall, you can slap a wheelchair symbol on the door. Never mind that I can't get *through* that door. Sure, someone may come along and let me in before I wet myself, but afterward I am apt to end up alone inside waiting for some other woman's full bladder to bring her to my rescue. Why couldn't the weight be removed, or the door hung so as to swing both ways, or an electric device installed to respond to the push of a button? Once inside, I may or may not be able to maneuver my wheelchair up to the appropriate stall (always at the far end), open that door, and fit inside. Almost without question, there won't be room for me to turn and close the door behind me. Good thing my bladder isn't uncommonly bashful, or all my labors would be in vain.

These arrangements presume that I'm self-locomoting, but when we travel with a manual chair, I'm not. George has to open the door, push me forward a bit so that I can make sure that no woman is hitching up her pantyhose in plain view, and then take me in. The occupants tend to be startled but gracious. If our roles were reversed (and plenty of women have to assist partners), the situation would be untenable, with all those men out in the open waving their members in the direction of the urinals. In England, this problem occurs much more rarely, since separate rooms, spacious and well-outfitted, are provided in most public places.

About now I can imagine you saying you don't know why I'm dwelling on this indelicate subject again. After all, people don't devote a lot of mental energy to using the bathroom; they just do it and get it over with. Precisely. Our society assumes that people want to take care of this bodily function themselves, in private and without a lot of bother. Many of us with disabilities require some assistance, but with the right facilities, we can maintain dignity for ourselves and those who care for us. Somebody has got to talk about toilets, even though Mother said not to, or the nondisabled will go right on rushing into and out of public rest rooms without even seeing the barriers. And whatever goes unseen goes unchanged.

My great concern is that, in an era when peevish voters press for a different "quick fix" with every election, unnerved legislators will jettison the Americans with Disabilities Act long before the new conditions it mandates can work more than superficial change in either the lives of the disabled or the attitudes of the nondisabled. Directives are essential until the standards they put into place come to seem so natural that behaviors are permanently altered; but such transformation is not going to occur in the couple of years between national elections, when one set of bums gets thrown out and another set sweeps in, promising to reverse whatever their predecessors put into place. Currently, governmental protection of the powerless is unfashionable, and in the tempestuous drive to get rid of "big government," I can

well imagine Congress proudly pitching ADA over-
board. I remember reading a passage in which William
F. Buckley, Jr., describing a visit to his mother, commented how sweet she always smelled, despite her de-
terioration in old age, and snapping to myself, "Well, of
course she smells sweet. A nurse looks after her twenty-
four hours a day. Put her in a county nursing home for a
week and see how sweet she smells." Power and privi-
lege dangerously insulate policy-makers from the real
needs of their constituents.

One day, it may seem as silly to build a structure
without a ramp as it would be to leave off a set of
steps today; but at the moment people must be told to
do so or they'll simply "forget." Legislation like ADA,
designed to establish the civil rights of a population
hitherto assumed to be a little less than kin, must counter centuries of habitual neglect, exclusion, and worse:
only half a century ago, after all, physical and mental
"defectives" were exterminated in Nazi Germany
alongside homosexuals and Jews. Historically, the
treatment of the disabled has generally stopped short
(by at least a couple of inches) of outright atrocity; and
most people in the United States would protest against
the torture and killing of a young mentally retarded
woman (although if she were instead raped by a group of
high-school students, at least some would rationalize
that boys will be boys and anyway she asked for and
even liked it).

"Why even bring up the subject of monstrosity?" my
husband asks when I condemn Nazi efforts to purge the

state of people with physical and mental defects. "No one will disagree with you there." He's right. I hope. At least, I would not expect anyone I'm likely to meet to view medical experimentation without consent, forced sterilization, or the slaughter of innocents (or any of the rest of us, for that matter) as anything but unconscionable violations of human rights. In this sense, I am not looking for argument, I assure you.

But I would expect—because I regularly encounter— the sort of socially hygienic attitudes toward people with disabilities that might have permitted otherwise compassionate human beings to acquiesce in, or at least to overlook, such desecration of human life. These attitudes may be held, often unawares, by people so well-meaning and scrupulous that they would be aghast to have their opinions associated, even tenuously, with the atrocities of an indubitably mad dictator obsessed with the purity of his "race."

Because the political conditions aren't equivalent, we can easily dismiss the underlying danger. "Why even mention behavior so bestial?" we say. "Nothing like that could ever happen here." The matter is not so simple, however. Human personality tends to retain common elements across time and geography and political regime, being fond of familiar surroundings and routines, defensive of friends and kin but suspicious of outsiders, morally righteous, intolerant of ambiguity, fearful of pain and death. We don't like unpleasantness, in whatever way it's culturally defined. We readily conform to existing social standards. We are insatiably curious. We are apt all but unwittingly to hold the lives of some among us cheap, even expendable.

And yes, things "like that" could happen—have happened—here. Black men with syphilis have gone untreated so that doctors could study the advance of the disease; civilians have been irradiated without caution while the military tested nuclear weapons; mental patients have been isolated, drugged, sunk into diabetic comas, immersed in icy baths, lobotomized. We like to believe that such outrages occurred in the benighted past, and many of these did, but without doubt something very like them is going on today, although so secretly that we may never hear about it until *this* has become the benighted past. Nevertheless, acts like these remain relatively rare, and once discovered, they are generally condemned as obvious violations of civil and/ or human rights.

In setting aside the matter of monstrous behaviors here, as I intend to do, I don't mean to deny or trivialize their occurrence. I simply have no experience of them, and in a society that professes to protect all its members, probably most other disabled people don't either. For the moment, what's important to me is not the outrageous but the ordinary: the normally unconscious attitudes that chill the social climate for people marked out by disability. Although these do not threaten bodily harm, they deplete and shrivel the spirit, leaving people whose resources may already be scanty enough hollowed out and sad. If you want people to assume responsibility for themselves (and this is what we should all want for each other, I think), you ought not to beat them into the emotional ground.

What is critical is an understanding of the realities disability imposes, and the only way finally to develop the necessary empathy is through knowing disabled individuals. Most nondisabled people I know are so driven by their own fears of damage and death that they dread contact, let alone interaction, with anyone touched by affliction of any kind, as my mother-in-law demonstrated, not for the first time, just the other night. When George and I were dropping her off at the retirement complex where she has lived for the past couple of years, she closed the evening on a plaintive note.

"It's always so good to get away from this place," she turned to me and sighed. "You know, over fifty percent of the people who live here now use wheelchairs or walkers or oxygen tanks. It's *so* depressing." She is the kind of woman who tends not to take an imaginative step outside her own skin, and apparently it never crossed her mind that she was directing her grievance at a woman tied down to the floor of her van in a wheelchair, who did not need to be told that she and her kind constitute a blight on the world's joy.

I think Mum's oblique point was not really to disparage cripples but to elicit the guilt without which she appears to think we'll stop inviting her out. Whatever the peculiarities of the encounter, however, I suspect that the attitude she expressed toward the disabled residents of The Cascades is so common that it wouldn't give most people pause. Users of assistive devices, unlike people with less observable disabilities (such as her own severely limited vision and hearing) are forced to parade their impediments, and these elicit a sorrowful or even indignant distaste in those who have to look at them. Ironically, I have found that elderly people are particularly intolerant of anyone who arouses such unpleasant feelings, so that one retirement community in Tucson expressly bans any occupant who uses even a cane, as though obliterating all signs of frailty will protect them from the falls and fractures to which each year makes them more vulnerable. How shattered those who choose to live in such a place must be when, after some bodily misadventure, they are cast out: old, ugly, ruined, *depressing*.

I have often felt constrained not to inflict my dreary condition upon the vigorous, as though I spoiled any party at which I showed up. As a rule, such pressure is tacit: the slide of an eye in any direction but mine, the exasperated sigh, ever so slight, at having to open a space for my wheelchair. Once, a taxi driver actually shouted at me that I should not be out riding around Providence in his cab but home where people like me belonged. I was furious but also, in a way, refreshed: he had come right out with the aversion that, in subtler forms, poisons the atmosphere like a fine gray mist, indiscernible but for the headache and lassitude it induces.

When, having noted the driver's number, I telephoned the city government to complain of my treatment, I learned that this driver had health problems of his own, faced possible surgery, might become permanently incapacitated. Although these particulars hardly excused his rudeness, they made me conscious for the first time that the people who seem most hostile to my presence are those most fearful of my fate. And since their fear keeps them emotionally distant from me, they are the ones least likely to learn that my life isn't half so dismal as they assume.

"I feel so *sorry* for them," George's mother went on about the old dears at The Cascades. As for so many women of her generation, even the faintest whiff of antagonism is impermissible; she certainly can't confront her anxiety, but pity lies above reproach. Some of these people may be pathetic, of course; like any population, people with disabilities have their share of woes. But reliance on assistive devices does not necessarily signify a wretched existence, as my beloved friend Ellie Robinett, tethered for years to an oxygen machine, has taught all of us whose lives she touches. She telephoned again the other day, as she does every year, to ask for help in organizing a fund-raiser for Tucson's Catholic Worker house, a woman who would—and perhaps will—expend her last breath on behalf of the homeless people Casa María feeds. I admire Ellie's generosity of spirit more than I can say, and I worry about her frail health; but I do not feel sorry for her. Nor would she want me to. She would expect me to save my pity for the drunken one-legged Vietnam veteran I met outside the drugstore yesterday; and even then, she would consider the emotion wasted unless I acted upon it to change the circumstances that have driven him to live on the streets.

"I always try to talk to them and cheer them up," Mum went on. "I hope I help them some." And then, as if suddenly remembering who she was talking to, she added brightly, "What do *you* think?"

"I think it depends on the person you're talking to," I told her. Voluble and warmhearted, she certainly could bring a welcome energy to a person feeling lonely and low. The trouble lies in her assuming first, that loneliness and low spirits plague everyone who has physical or mental limitations, and second, that whenever these feelings prevail, a person must be jollied out of them. I for one have a horror of cheer-mongers, which I associate with an evening more than a quarter of a century ago when I was an inmate at Metropolitan State Hospital and a group of hairdressers brought us refreshments and little gifts and music for a Christmas party. They meant well, I know, I knew even then, but the recollection of their wary eyes above their dogged smiles, their stiff bodies dancing us around the linoleum of the cavernous day room, mortifies me to this day.

To know that one arouses dismay and fear and pity simply sickens the spirit of anyone, whether sound of limb and mind or not. One is tempted to withdraw altogether, at least from the company of "normals," so as to avoid the indignity; but disappearance from the scene, however welcome to both parties, won't lead to change. It is not, after all, entirely the fault of people without disabilities that they don't know how to treat those of us with. Until rather recently, the lack of access and assistive technology, combined with social opprobrium, kept many of us out of public view. What intercourse occurred was marked by distance, restraint, even condescension; it was certainly not a communion of equals. The village I grew up in had its "idiot," a retarded hunchback named Sam. He came and went freely among us, but children and adults alike made fun of him behind his back, and no one, except perhaps his aging aunts, "knew" him.

If I want people to grow accustomed to my presence, and to view mine as an ordinary life, less agreeable in some of its particulars than theirs but satisfying over all, then I must routinely roll out among them. Inevitably, my emergence produces some strain. I must be "on" all the time, since people seldom glance down to my height and so tend to walk into me as though I were immaterial. Most who notice me are willing to help, and I never spurn an offer. Proving independence is a big issue with some disabled people, who will snap, "I can do it myself!" rather than permit so much as a door to be opened, but this attitude is often misinterpreted as churlishness (of which my Yankee grandmother would have heartily disapproved), and anyway I can use all the help I can get.

Of course, would-be helpers must be taught how; wrangling me into or out of a coat without detaching my arms requires a heroic blend of ingenuity and patience, not to mention the communication skills of a

United Nations ambassador, from helper and helpee alike. They must also be dissuaded tactfully when their efforts are worthless; pushing my electric wheelchair, for example, has no effect, since the wheels lock automatically whenever I stop. The pedagogical role required can wear thin. Sometimes I just want others to *know*, magically, that I need a paper towel from the dispenser above my head when I've washed my hands or that, even though a dazzling array of bottles is within my grasp, I want the brand of shampoo on the top shelf. I get weary to the point of weeping of the sound of my own voice: "Would you please? . . ."

This, however, is my own problem. The mark of self-reliance, for me, is not whether or not I open a door for myself but whether I accept the burden of my limitations. For the truth is that, regardless of structural and attitudinal modifications, I am never going to be entirely at ease in the world. Unless paradise is paved into a parking lot, most of the earth's surface is going to be too rough for my wheelchair. The top shelves of supermarkets will remain forever beyond my reach. I will never mingle at cocktail parties, since I can't juggle a drink and my joystick at the same time, and besides I get claustrophobic down among the milling bellies and buttocks. I won't dance again. To some, for reasons outside my control, I will always be a figure of pity, scorn, despair. "You're so brave," they will go on exclaiming, as though only true grit could prod a person through a life as loathsome as mine.

These are my realities, and some of them nearly break

my heart. Some of them don't. I will never wield a mop again, after all, or scrub another toilet bowl. My grief is selective. But it is not the world's task to assuage whatever genuine sorrows darken my spirit. I know this. I think most people with disabilities do. In asking that the entrance to a building be ramped, that the numbers on an elevator panel be brailled, that emergency services be equipped to communicate with people who cannot hear or speak clearly, no one expects all impediments to be miraculously whisked away. In insisting that others view our lives as ample and precious, we are not demanding that they be made perfect.

There are rewards for making the world physically and emotionally accessible to all people, including benefits that accrue to society as a whole. The more perspectives that can be brought to bear on human experience, even from the slant of a wheelchair or a hospital bed, or through the ears of a blind person or the fingers of someone who is deaf, the richer that experience becomes. If it is both possible and pleasant for me and my kind to enter, the world will become a livelier place. You'll see.

Freeing Choices

A SEPTEMBER Sunday morning, still and hot. George and I munch our ritual scones with strawberry jam as we leaf through the *New York Times* and half listen to Weekend Edition on NPR. An interview comes on that I begin to heed more closely: a discussion of the increasingly common practice of using amniocentesis to determine the sex of a fetus, followed by abortion if the parents don't want the sort they've begun. What they generally want, as parents have done from time immemorial, is a boy.

The person being interviewed plainly shares my distaste for sexual selectivity. But the way she articulates it brings me up short. "Sex," she tells her interlocuter emphatically, "is not a birth defect."

"That sort of statement strikes a chill straight through my heart," I say to George, who has begun to listen more closely, too. He looks puzzled for a moment and then responds: "Oh. Yes. I can see how it might. I never thought of it that way."

Not very many people would. The implicit argument appears self-evident: the use of abortion to fulfill the desire for a male (or female) child is impermissible, but the same use to prevent an imperfect one is not merely legitimate but, many would argue, socially responsible. As a defective myself, however, I have some doubts.

Although mine was not a birth defect, some evidence suggests a genetic predisposition toward MS, and one day—perhaps even quite soon—this may be detectable. What then? What if, I find myself wondering, such a test had been devised more than half a century ago? Suppose a genetic counselor had said to my mother, "Your baby will be born healthy, and she will probably remain so throughout childhood. But at some point, perhaps in her twenties, she is likely to develop a chronic incurable degenerative disease of the central nervous system. She may go blind. She may not be able to speak. Her bladder and bowels may cease to function normally. She may become incapable of walking or even of moving at all. She could experience tingling, numbness, or intractable pain. In the end, she might have to be fed, bathed, dressed and undressed, turned over in bed, as helpless as an infant." What would Mother have done then? What should she have done?

I don't know. Morally, I feel a lot more confident asking questions than answering them. What I do know, from my own circumstances, is that I am glad Mother never faced the option to "spare" me my fate, as she might have felt obliged to do. I simply cannot say—have never been able to say, even at my most depressed, when I have easily enough wished myself dead—that I wish I had never been born. Nor do I believe that MS has poisoned my existence. Plenty of people find my life unappealing, I know. To be truthful, it doesn't altogether appeal to me. But a good scone with a cup of hot coffee does much to set things right.

I know I am lucky. There are conditions crueler than MS, including many birth defects, and some of these are already detectable by amniocentesis and ultrasound. Suppose—and I'm being far less speculative here than I was in imagining my own mother—that a woman learns that her fetus has spina bifida. The degree of disability may be impossible to predict, but the risks, she is told, include intellectual impairment, bladder and bowel dysfunction, repeated infections, and the inability to walk. Bright, healthy, and active herself, the woman strains to imagine what quality a life thus impaired might possess. Such a child can adapt to her circumstances, of course, and grow into an energetic and resourceful woman like my friend Martha, now in her sixties, married, the moderator of her own radio show.

Even if persuaded of this potentiality, the mother still must decide whether she is emotionally and financially equipped for such an undertaking, with access to medical care and educational programs, reliable assistance from the child's father, a supportive community, a flexible attitude toward surprises and obstacles, and an indefatigable sense of humor. You can't decide that you're in the middle of a great book, and anyway you're sick unto death of the four-hour catheterization schedule, and the kid's bladder can damned well wait a couple of hours till you're more in the mood. Caring for children, even undamaged ones, never ceases, and in our society mothers are customarily expected to provide or arrange it. Much as I admire the mothers of variously disabled children I have known—and much as I believe their extraordinary qualities to derive, at least in part, from the rigors of their lives—I could not blame a woman who chose not to test her mettle in this way.

If I make her appear to be choosing in a social vacuum, I do so because, in a society where the rearing of even a healthy child is not viewed as a community undertaking, where much-touted "family values" are always ascribed to the nuclear and not the human family, the parents of a disabled child will find themselves pretty much on their own. If they are lucky enough to have health insurance, the insurer, whose goal is to maximize shareholders' profits rather than the well-being of patients, is not about to spring for a $7,000 power wheelchair that would enable a child with muscular dystrophy to mingle independently with his classmates on an almost equal "footing," though it might provide $425 for a manual wheelchair to be pushed by an attendant (which it would not pay for). A school system, underfunded by screaming taxpayers, is not likely to procure a Kurtzweil machine that would permit its blind students to "read" their own textbooks. Unless they are wealthy, Mom and Dad do the pushing, the reading, and whatever other extra duties are required, on top of their jobs and their care for any other children in the family.

"Eric and I plan to have only a couple of children," my daughter tells me, contemplating the start of a family. "Why should we expend our resources on a damaged one?" A plausible point, as I have come to expect from this most clearheaded of young women. And in fact, as she knows, her father and I took great care to avoid conceiving another child after her younger brother was born in distress because of Rh incompatibility. After a couple of blood exchanges, he recovered, but we were told that another baby would likely be damaged, perhaps gravely, by the antibodies in my blood. I was no more eager to raise a deformed or retarded child than Anne is. I might have chosen an abortion if contraception had failed.

But then I think of my godson, the product of contraceptive failure, who shares with his sister a possibly unique genetic condition that has caused severe visual impairment in them both. Many seeing people have a dread of blindness so overwhelming that they might well consider abortion if such a defect could be detected (as it could not in this case). But these are otherwise ideal children—healthy, smart, funny, confident, affectionate—and I think they're going to become terrific adults. The problem is that if you eliminate one flaw, you throw out the whole complicated creature, and my world would be a poorer place without Michael and Megan.

Obviously, I don't have an unambiguous answer to

this dilemma. I don't think one exists. I do feel certain, in view of the human propensity for exploiting whatever techniques we can devise with virtually no regard for consequences, that more and more people will choose, either for their own reasons or in response to the social pressure not to produce "unnecessary" burdens, to terminate pregnancies so as to avoid birth defects (and to select for sex as well). This development won't eradicate people with disabilities, of course: birth trauma, accidental injury, and disease will continue to create them from those who started out as even the healthiest fetuses. What it will do is to make their social position even more marginal by emphasizing that no one with the power to choose would ever have permitted them to exist. Their own choice to survive will seem suspect. *We're doing everything we can to exterminate your kind*, the social message will read, *and we'd get rid of you too if only we knew how*. No one will ever say this. No one will have to.

This mute message—that one is an accident that ought not to have happened—is communicated again, in the issues surrounding the other end of life, by the current movement to legally protect the "right to die." This phrase always strikes me as a little odd, since the right to do a thing presupposes the option not to do it. Although one's conception and birth are chancy at best (will a sperm reach the egg, and if so, which one? will the egg implant? will the fetus reach viability?), one's death is absolutely not; and legislation in such matters seems wildly inappropriate. Human beings have never been able to leave one another's bodies alone, however, but seem compelled to regulate even their most private moments, and so I suppose it is inevitable that some of them are going to set out to protect one's legal right to do what one can't help doing anyway.

The phrase "right to die" is shorthand, of course, and seems considerably less reductive when spelled out: what is generally being called for by right-to-die advocates is the protection of one's freedom to choose the time and circumstances of one's own death and to receive assistance from willing accomplices if necessary. I am as adamantly pro-choice in this matter as I am with regard to abortion; but as with abortion, the question of "choice" here is vastly more complex than politicians, legislators, and religious fundamentalists make it. Their (self-)delegated task is to reduce the rich ambiguities of life to a set of binaries—us/them, law/ transgression, right/wrong. The labels vary but the underlying aim is constant—so that we can all stretch out on the couch every Saturday afternoon in front of some quintessentially binary sports contest rather than on a moral rack. Just as your team wins or loses, you either vote for a candidate or you don't, who upon election either does or does not enact certain promised laws, which you either break or obey, and in the end, depending on the choices made, both you and your representative go to Heaven or to Hell.

For absolutists, the "right to die" issue is as indisputable as abortion: killing oneself, or helping another to die, is murder; although the first act is humanly unpunishable, the second ought to be penalized to the full extent of the law, which, in most states, requires that the perpetrator receive assistance in dying by electrocution, suffocation, or lethal injection. Oh well, "a foolish consistency is the hobgoblin of little minds," and all that. Absolutists come in more than one stripe, however (though such a pluralistic view would be repudiated by absolutists themselves), and some of those who crusade to pass legislation permitting assisted suicide seem just as scarily single-minded as their opponents: Jack Kevorkian, "Dr. Death," the principal figure among them.

My own relationship to suicide renders this an unusually vexed topic for me. I have suffered from clinical depression for several decades now, and although not all depressives become suicidal during an episode, I do. I have tried to kill myself more than once, and the last time I so nearly succeeded, taking an overdose of antidepressant medication, that I am unlikely to fail another time. Thus, I must monitor myself ceaselessly for symptoms that signal a downward spiral in order to seek timely treatment. I have spent a good deal of my life struggling to deny myself the death to which activists would like to guarantee me the right.

To complicate matters, I am as vulnerable as the next person to the ordinary situational depression that surges in response to painful life events. The triggers vary from person to person—a broken friendship, a miscarriage, divorce, the departure of children, even a failed exam or the death of a pet—but almost all of us have endured at least brief periods of sleeplessness, loss of appetite, panic attacks, distractability, or ill-defined malaise following some personal catastrophe. Although my own situation gladdens more than it pains me, it does contain some grimmish elements, especially the threat of my husband's death. And because I am a suicidal depressive, I respond to this threat by wanting to kill myself.

A couple of years ago, George began to experience severe bowel problems, and because his melanoma had last recurred in his small bowel, these strongly suggested a relapse. Although I have always known that this may happen at some point, knowledge is no proof against terror, and I went instantly into a tailspin that very nearly carried me over the precipice of panic into the eternal abyss. I procured twice the amount of the medication that had nearly killed me the last time, and I began to plan: "Some afternoon while George is still teaching, so as to have plenty of time," I wrote in my journal. "Drink a beer to relax. Spread out an underpad to avoid soiling the bed. Lie down on it. That way I can't chicken out—once down, I can't get up again. Put on the white-noise machine. Go to sleep forever." Fortunately, I've been in the depression business long enough now to remain a little skeptical about my urges. "It would be stupid to die for no reason," I noted, "so I suppose I should wait until the tumor has been located." That shred of rationality held me back long enough to learn that this time George had not cancer but an antibiotic-induced colitis, and we have both lived to tell the tale.

My intimacy with self-destructive urges leads me to question the term "rational" suicide, which right-to-die proponents use supposedly to distinguish the death they have in mind from the one I have approached so closely. Suicide appears imperative only when one loses sight of all other alternatives (and there is always at least one other). Since hopelessness is a distinctive symptom of depression, which is an emotional disorder, actions carried out in a despairing state seem to me intrinsically irrational. This last time I clung to some shreds of reason, which saved me.

I also remembered my son-in-law's words during a family discussion of the precarious future, his voice flat and slightly muffled as it can get with strong feeling: "I think it would be very inconsiderate of you to kill yourself." If there's anything that chagrins me, it's acting stupid or inconsiderate. Better I should stay alive.

Seriously, consideration for others is one of the motives often expressed by people who argue for the license to end their own lives: the desire, sometimes quite desperate, not to be a "burden" on others. Perhaps as a legacy of the rugged individualism that fueled colonial settlement, our society has developed a peculiar structure, in which we create small units that, after a certain amount of time, break and expel even smaller fragments who will form their own similarly friable units: children can't wait to escape their parents, who sometimes can't wait to be escaped, and have families of their "own."

The parent who becomes more than a peripheral part of the new constellation, especially one who because of incapacity requires a child's assistance, is considered an intrusion.

Shucking the previous generation in this way doesn't appear to have a practical basis. I mean, we hardly live under the conditions that forced the Eskimos to float their aged and ill off on ice floes in order to conserve scarce resources. The hardships entailed in keeping three or even four generations under one roof are, I think, psychological rather than material. And, as our staggering divorce rate makes clear, we are not, as a society, tolerant of the kind of psychological hardship I have in mind, caused by the tensions that inevitably arise between people living in intimacy. Our notion of satisfactory relationships is incurably romantic in the least wholesome sense of the phrase. We are so bombarded in the media by various and garbled messages about intimate interactions—from the pictorial rapture of a perfume advertisement to the pop-psych-speak of experts on television talk shows to horrific newspaper accounts of domestic abuse—that instead of accepting ordinary conflict as one of the fixed, though less agreeable features, of the human condition, we label it "bad," "sick," and damp it down as best we can, sticking the latest Arnold Schwarzenegger movie into the VCR, pouring a drink or popping a Prozac, heading out for a day at the mall, filing for divorce, whatever it takes to disengage from the maddening other. Or we explode, savaging or even killing the source of irritation.

No wonder the presence of another can seem a burden. No wonder some people would rather die than play such a role.

Many years ago, when I first became active in securing low-income housing for my community, I asked a friend from Israel, whose descriptions of various social programs there had impressed me, about housing for the elderly. He looked a little puzzled, and thinking he didn't understand the term, though his English was excellent, I explained the concept.

"Yes, I understand," he said. "We don't have any."

"What do you do with your old people, then?"

"They live with their families."

This notion was hardly foreign to me, since my grandmother had lived with us from the time I was nine; but the idea that an entire society could accept such an arrangement seemed strange indeed. Even though my own experience proved the contrary, I assumed that each generation naturally desired to be quit of the other, except perhaps at holidays, as soon as possible.

The horror of functioning as one of Job's afflictions can be so overwhelming that it obscures the needs and desires of others. That day years back when, panic-stricken at George's impending death, I told my neurologist that I didn't want my children to take care of me because "that's not who I want to be in their lives," Dr. Johnson merely nodded, and we went on to discuss home help, Meals on Wheels, assisted-living arrangements in retirement communities, and other alternatives to the nursing home that evokes dread in just about all of us. I had then, and still have, no idea whether Anne (and now her husband) would consider taking me into their lives, and how burdensome they would find me if they did, but that's just the point: *I have no idea.* Anne was sitting right there, but I blurted what I thought she'd be relieved to hear—that she'd never be saddled with me—without taking the time to ask. At that moment, in the presence of a woman we scarcely knew, both of us distraught over George's illness, we could hardly have delved into the matter. But I could have said, should have said, something open-ended: "I don't know about living with my children. We haven't yet talked about it." Instead, I played Boss Mom, as I have done all too often, decreeing that only what I wanted could be done.

What I wanted—and what I think all of us want who demand the right to die on our own terms—was to maintain a sense of control. Even more than the dread of becoming a burden, helplessness triggers in us a manic terror that things are slipping from our grasp, and I was feeling more impotent than I had ever felt before. A few months earlier, a severe fall had signaled the dreaded end of my walking days. Since then, I had watched George's flesh melt mysteriously away, and now the bony remains huddled like jetsam on a hospital bed, tubes in his arms, his nose, his penis, and nothing I could do would bring him back. These circumstances struck me as intolerable, and I wanted the right to refuse them permanently and irreversibly.

I still do. I want to be the one in charge of my life, including its end, and I want to be able to enlist someone to help me terminate it if I choose "rational" suicide. I have a friend, a doctor whom I admire deeply, who has told me about assisting a patient, irreversibly ill and on a ventilator, to die: listening carefully to the man's clear and repeated requests, calling together his family for their last goodbyes, administering a shot of morphine to ease his passage, turning off the ventilator, remaining with him until he had gone. I would hope to find someone as brave and compassionate if I were to make a similar appeal.

But I would not seek out Dr. Kevorkian or any other crusader for euthanasia, because people who act on principle are likely to sacrifice the individual for the agenda, which is frequently shaped by their own, often deeply buried, presuppositions about what constitutes an acceptable life. Doctors despise disease, or else they wouldn't become doctors, and I have heard of those who couldn't bring themselves to tell a patient she or he had multiple sclerosis because the diagnosis seemed too horrible to bear. Isn't a doctor suffering from this kind of anxiety all too likely to tell me: "You have MS? Of course you want to die! Here, let me write you a prescription so you can peacefully end it all."

In other words, the social construction of disability which makes me uneasy about urging abortion to prevent defective children disturbs me here, too. Behind the view of death as a "right" to be seized and defended lurks the hidden assumption that some lives are not worth living and that damaged creatures may be put out of their misery. True, all kinds of safeguards would be put into place to ensure that only the person doing the dying could make the ultimate decision; but no amount of regulation can eliminate the subtle pressure to end a life perceived by others to be insufferable. If, ideally, I ought never to have born, and if my dependent existence creates a burden on those who must care for me, then don't I have not merely the right but the obligation to die? How can I honorably choose otherwise?

My purpose in raising questions about abortion and euthanasia is not to condemn these procedures, which I believe ought to be freely available, in strict privacy, to any fully informed person who elects them. In fact, I would educate doctors more, and regulate them less, so that they and their patients could explore options, reach decisions, and take action without intrusion. My concern is that these issues be confronted in such a way as to create a social climate in which people with disabilities perceive life to be an honorable choice. And that means sending the social message that disabled people are valued and valuable, precious even, by investing, financially and emotionally, in institutions and practices that help them out.

Everybody, well or ill, disabled or not, imagines a boundary of suffering and loss beyond which, she or he is certain, life will no longer be worth living. I know that I do. I also know that my line, far from being scored in stone, has inched across the sands of my life: at various times, I could not possibly do without long walks on the beach or rambles through the woods; use a cane, a brace, a wheelchair; stop teaching; give up driving; let someone else put on and take off my underwear. One at a time, with the encouragement of others, I have taken each of these (highly figurative) steps. Now I believe my limit to lie at George's death, but I am prepared to let it move if it will. When I reach the wall, I think I'll know. Meanwhile, I go on being, now more than ever, the woman I once thought I could never bear to be.

I cannot excuse or condemn those women with MS, less crippled than I, who sought out Dr. Kevorkian's services. They had their lines. They may have lacked adequate support: familial, medical, psychological, spiritual. I can, however, defend the human right to choose actions that the nondisabled find unfathomable and perhaps even indecent. If a woman, upon learning that her fetus has spina bifida, may choose abortion, then she ought also to feel free to decide, without apology, to bear and rear the child, certain that she will have the same access to medical care and educational programs that a nondisabled child enjoys. If, after consulting with family, spiritual counselors, and medical personnel, a diabetic with gangrenous legs may ask for an easeful death, he should also be fully supported in his decision to live on as an amputee, confident that he can continue to work, shop, attend church, take his wife out for dinner and a movie, just as he has always done. Only in a society that respects, and enables, these choices are atrocities against the disabled truly unthinkable.

"But provisions for these people cost *money*," fiscal conservatives squeal, "and why should *I* pay for someone else's misfortune?" Because that's what human beings do: take care of one another. "But we can't *afford* it." In my experience, this argument is most commonly made by those who mean they can't afford both high taxes or charitable donations and membership in the country club or a winter home in Florida, but never mind. The perception of scarcity is highly subjective, and if you believe yourself on the doorsill of the poorhouse, nothing I say can comfort your fears (though, as Thomas Friedman once pointed out in an editorial in the *New York Times*, a short trip to Africa might have a salutory effect).

Let me point out, instead, being something of a fiscal conservative myself, that we're not talking huge amounts here, nothing like the billions squandered on Star Wars and the B-2 stealth bomber, which plenty of people believed we could afford. If the money is spent wisely, it will constitute not a drain but an investment. Thousands of people with disabilities are already productive citizens; with adequate funds for medical care and research into preventable and treatable conditions, education, structural modifications, and adaptive equipment, we can create thousands more. They will support themselves! They will pay taxes! They will make charitable donations! Their potential contributions to culture are impossible to gauge. (Alexander Pope and Toulouse-Lautrec were hunchbacks, after all; Milton went blind; Beethoven, deaf, and so on, and so on. We can ill afford to kill off our geniuses, and every live birth holds such promise.) They will weave into the social fabric important strands of tenacity, patience, and ingenuity. We will all be glad they were born, I think. We will be glad they chose to live on.

Young and Disabled

LUNCHTIME. Your favorite café. Blinking away the dust and glare of the street, your gaze falls on a woman at the corner table. Her dark hair swings softly against cheeks as flawless as porcelain, and her chin rests on the slender fingers of one hand. In her beige silk blouse and ivory linen suit, she has the crisp appearance of someone who holds a powerful job and does it well. She leans forward to say something to the man across from her, and when he throws his head back with a deep laugh, her eyes sparkle.

Yourself, you're having a bad-hair day, and a zing up your calf tells you you're going to have to dash into the drugstore for a new pair of pantyhose before returning to your office, where the world's most boring report lies on your desk, still only half read. You stayed awake half the night worrying whether your boyfriend will take the job he's been offered in Denver, and now your brain feels as soggy as a fallen log under a thick layer of moss. But your stomach is rumbling, so you head for a table in the back.

As you pass the woman, you see with a start that she's sitting in a wheelchair. "Oh, the poor thing!" you think. "How courageous she is to fix herself up and get out of the house on a day as hot as this. And what a thoughtful man—her brother, it must be—treating her to lunch to cheer her up." In an instant, your mossy brain has dredged up an entirely new creature. The person you first noticed—the glamorous career woman enjoying a flirtation over lunch—is no more real, of course, than this pitiful invalid putting a brave face on her misery. Both are projections of your own imagination—your desires, your dreads. But because you admire the first, you're more likely to want to know her; the second, because she makes you uneasy, will remain a stranger.

The "you" I refer to is as much my young self as she is anyone else. In those days, I knew almost no one with a disability. When I was a child, one of my uncles had become partially paralyzed by polio, but he moved to Florida and I seldom saw him after that. Although two of my college classmates had been disabled, one quite severely, and I remember watching in wonder as she maneuvered her crutches over paths made treacherous by the New England winter, I didn't happen to know—or did I avoid knowing?—either of them well. Those were the days before buildings were ramped, elevators installed, and bathrooms modified for accessibility, and I can't imagine how complicated and exhausting and downright dangerous their lives must have been. No wonder relatively few disabled people ventured out into the world.

Then I became one of them. When my neurologist diagnosed my multiple sclerosis, he told me that I had a "normal" life expectancy. But, he didn't have to tell me, I wouldn't have a "normal" life, not the one I had prepared myself to live. I was going to be "disabled," more severely as time went on, and I had no idea how to live such a life. Could I go on teaching, and if so, would anybody want to hire me? Would my husband still find me sexually attractive, and could he accept my increasing need for help? Would my children resent having a mother who couldn't do everything that other mothers could? How would I survive if they all abandoned me? Did I even want to live to find out the answers to these questions?

As such questions suggest, I subscribed to the major social myths about the "disabled woman": that she lacks the health or competence to hold a job; that no man could want her or care for her, either physically or emotionally; that disability can only damage, never enhance, friendships and family relationships; that suicide is an understandable, even a rational, response to physical impairment, rather than the symptom of depression it is known to be in nondisabled people. Above all, I felt permanently exiled from "normality." Whether imposed by self or society, this outsider status—and not the disability itself—constitutes the most daunting barrier for most people with physical impairments, because it, even more than flights of steps or elevators without braille, prevents them from participating fully in the ordinary world, where most of life's satisfactions dwell.

Gradually, I stopped thinking of myself as an outcast, and over the years I have watched the social barriers crumbling as well. As technological advances permit disabled people to travel, study, and work, and as the media incorporate their pictures and stories into articles, advertising, television programs, and films, their presence becomes more familiar and less frightening. Many of them are eager to promote this process, as *Glamour* magazine discovered by asking readers with disabilities to write about their histories and the effects that their physical circumstances have had on their work, their friendships, and their love lives. Letters and faxes flooded in from several hundred women (and a handful of men), ranging in age from sixteen to eighty-five but most in their twenties and thirties, who were "intrigued," "excited," and "thrilled" at being asked to emerge from the shadows. Having the chance to collate these for an article I wrote for the magazine, I became charmed by the frankness, grit, and good humor these women displayed.

The challenge in compressing their replies—many of them covering several closely typed or handwritten pages—lay in fairly representing their diversity. Their disabilities varied so widely that it was difficult—even deceptive—to generalize about such women, who may have less in common with each other than they do with some nondisabled women and who may even be made uneasy by women with disabilities different from their own. As Peggy Merriman, who was diagnosed with multiple sclerosis when she was nineteen, protested, "The general public seems to have an easier time (or simply unconsciously prefers) dealing with people with disabilities by lumping us all together and assuming that we all have the same problems and, what is worse, that *all* we deal with or have in our life is our disability." But defining someone solely in terms of what she cannot do tends to distort her life: "I feel I have been neatly tucked into a category with no room to move," wrote twenty-one-year-old Naomi Passman, whose legs were paralyzed in infancy by a spinal tumor, but "the last thing I need are limits!" I hope that, as these women speak, "disability" will emerge as one element of their complicated personalities and not as a confining category.

Nevertheless, as every woman who wrote to *Glamour* has long since found out, breaking free of a category doesn't abolish the realities of the disability itself, which may include weakness, fatigue, deformity, physical pain, bouts of illness, and reliance on technical assistance like crutches, wheelchairs, or hearing aids. In a society that equates "vitality" and "beauty" with physical soundness, a disabled woman must come to terms with serious shortcomings often earlier and even more urgently than others. In this process, these women have learned from experience what many their age understand only intellectually, that life itself is imperfect: the best qualified person doesn't always get the job, the most loving heart doesn't always find a mate. Although a few responded to such knowledge with bitterness or apathy, most seemed to take it as a challenge. Their lives might not be "perfect" by conventional social standards, but they were determined to live productively and passionately anyway.

Those who were disabled from birth, by conditions like spina bifida and cerebral palsy, had to cope with being "different" during the time when social conformity seems most compelling. For many of them, childhood was anything but carefree, since they often faced both painful medical treatments and the taunts of "normal" schoolmates. Their reactions to their situations often diverged, however, as revealed by the responses of two women with osteogenesis imperfecta, a genetic disorder that causes bones to fracture very easily. "My parents were somewhat over-protective, which is highly understandable," wrote Felicia Wells Williams, a young African American woman who was born with several ribs and both arms already broken. "However, some of their apprehensiveness about my 'fragile' condition rubbed off on me. As a young child, I was told to be careful and think of the consequences of my actions. So I became fearful of certain things—heights, falling down stairs, etc. I spent a lot of my childhood being a spectator—watching others have fun." Konie Gardner, with the same diagnosis, recalled that her parents assigned her Saturday chores just like her five brothers and sisters and gave her every opportunity to try whatever she wanted. "I was always an accepted kid in the neighborhood, too, and even though I could not physically participate in many of the games, etc., I was an enthusiastic spectator and never felt left out by anyone." Whereas one felt she was missing the fun, the other had fun just watching.

Many received the kind of encouragement Kim Silvey reported: born with dislocated hips that required ten operations while she was growing up, Kim "wasn't one to hide and not be seen by anybody," thanks to her parents, who "instilled in me confidence and the belief that I could do anything I wanted, and that's the attitude I grew up with and the one I still hold today." She added, "It would have been so easy for them to coddle me and try to keep me out of the 'evil eye' of the world and to try to shelter me from the pain others could inflict upon me. I credit my being who I am today to my parents' unwillingness to hide me because I didn't fit the 'normal' mold."

Even those with supportive parents often found other children cruel. "With a toe first walking style, slurred speech and nearly no fine motor coordination, I was not what anyone considered popular," recalled Barbara McGuire, thirty-four, born with cerebral palsy and educated in regular classes. "I was the first to get 'cooties' (call me if you don't remember this social disease of elementary school kids); the last to get rid of them; the first to get teased; the last to get picked in gym." From early on, "boys were terribly mean," and by junior high school girls were, too, "to impress the boys." Only after entering an all-girls' high school did she begin to make lifelong friends.

The struggle for approval from nondisabled peers can

have humorous consequences, as Juli Delzer, born with a 60 percent hearing loss in both ears, revealed. As a child, "I was so painfully shy about my deafness that it was embarrassing to let people know that I couldn't hear. I came up with what I call 'deaf answers.' If someone asked me a question that I didn't hear, I would answer with 'yes,' 'no,' or 'I don't know,' hoping that I had covered the bases and given an appropriate answer. This didn't work so well when I moved to a new school. In gym class one day, someone turned around to ask, 'What's your name?' To which I answered, 'I don't know.'" Now, planning to do small animal husbandry in the Peace Corps before she begins veterinary school, Juli has grown self-assured enough to give up these "deaf answers," but still, she wrote, "I am very aware of my handicap in relationships with men. They can't whisper sweet nothings in my ear because I would be forced to look at them and whisper back, 'What?'"

In addition to a sense of humor, pride did much to carry these women through their awkward childhood years. "On the day I received my first hearing aid, when I was nine years old, my doctor assured me my long hair would easily hide it," wrote Madeline Cohen, a student at Stanford Law School who was also born deaf. "In response, I pulled my hair into a pony tail and walked out of his office with my nose in the air."

The dependencies of childhood—for nurture, instruction, and approval from adults—were often especially hard for these women to outgrow, though virtually all of them appear to have succeeded. The transition was not always a happy one. "As a child I was very

much treated like a cossetted princess: dressed in beautiful clothes and sheltered from the outside world,"
wrote thirty-two-year-old Karyna Laroche, whose muscular dystrophy requires her to rely on caregivers for virtually all her needs. An outstanding student, she attended a special school for disabled students until, at
thirteen, she transferred to a regular high school, where
"I finally realized just how different I was from other
kids, how being disabled was only considered cute and
socially acceptable when one is young, otherwise it is a
social embarrassment." The shock was so great that, despite outward success, "inwardly I only wanted to die.
My first suicide attempt occurred at the age of 16 and
suicide plans and attempts continued until I turned 30."
Only then did she discover "just how lucky I was to be
living on my own (which I love), to have great friends,
and to have the chance to build a life based on my needs
rather than on others' expectations of me."

More often, simply entering adulthood brought a new
rush of self-confidence. When Michele Anne Hope
Micheline, a student at Emory University whose spina
bifida, though relatively mild, has necessitated a number of operations on her left foot, developed a severe ul-
cer on her normal right foot during her freshman year,
the doctors wanted to amputate the infected bone. "I realized," she reported, "almost like a slap on my face,
that I was old enough to tell them that [surgery] was
NOT how I wanted it. I had a right to say no, to get a second opinion. To grasp my life." Finding a doctor in
whom she had complete confidence, who was able to
save all but half of her big toe, and having her left foot

reconstructed, she assumed responsibility for her own well-being. She has come to terms with the fact that she will always have to deal with a disability and that doctors, though useful, "can't give you a perfect foot. They can't give you what God didn't. You have to find a substitute within yourself for what you are lacking."

Some respondents had already reached adulthood when, like me, they developed a disabling disease or else were injured in skiing, motorcycle, automobile, or on-the-job accidents—even, in one case, a tornado. After I learned that I had multiple sclerosis, the transitions I had to make, involving the development of a new sense of who I was and what I was good for, required mourning the loss of the "old me" as I confronted a new one who seemed like a stranger. The active young wife and mother faded: no longer could I run after my young children or dance with their father. When my waist-length hair grew too heavy for my weakening hands to wash and brush, I had to cut it off, and suddenly I felt no longer carefree and sexy but practical and matronly. With degenerative conditions like mine, self-definition may have to be revised in this way again and again as new limitations develop.

For those struck by sudden catastrophe, the need to adjust may have come instantly, but the process itself took time. Muffy Davis was fifteen, training to be an Olympic ski racer, when an accident on the slopes left her paralyzed from mid-chest down. "It always amazed me when people would say, 'I don't know how you do it. I could never do it!' You don't have a choice, you just do it! What most people don't realize is that they would do this also. They see a disabled person and immediately put themselves in that person's shoes. What they don't realize is that disabled person didn't just get to wherever she was right away. It took time and grieving, but slowly day by day she got better, and eventually she was right back to attacking life, like she had been before her disability." After graduating from Stanford and before beginning medical school, Muffy plans to "give myself a shot at ski racing again, this time as a disabled athlete. I don't want to have any regrets when I get older." Thanks to adaptive sports equipment, such a goal is within her reach.

Whether gradually or suddenly, disabilities that occur in adulthood require revisions of identity that can yield fresh insight, as Madeline Cohen, who has a degenerative retinal disease in addition to her 85 to 90 percent hearing loss, discovered during a three-week Outward Bound experience after college graduation. "Had I stumbled over your disability survey announcement a few years ago, I might have continued flipping through the magazine with little more than a passing glance," she wrote, because she did not grow up defining herself as disabled. On Outward Bound, she encountered "a virtual assault of obstacles. Not the least of these was learning to recognize my limitations, voice them to my group members, and accept assistance from those around me. The latter was (and remains) the most difficult." As the days went by, she came to perceive that "everyone in my group carried special needs [one, for instance, was terrified of heights, and Madeline was able to talk him through a scary climb] and that by accepting assistance, I was acknowledging my participation in the cooperative human endeavor. Since that time, I have been learning to define myself as a 'person with a disability.'"

Regardless of when their disabled lives began or what pattern they have followed, all the respondents confronted the same issues in the "cooperative human endeavor" known as life as did their nondisabled peers. "People seem surprised and often patronizing when they find out I have a job and a social life," wrote Peggy Merriman, who works for a nonprofit agency assisting released prisoners, as though disability drained away all the interest taken by normal young women (and some of us who are not so young!) in finding meaningful work and developing personal relationships. On the contrary! Despite the enormous variety of their experiences, virtually all the respondents devoted much of their energy to the issues surrounding career and love.

A number were still undergraduate or graduate students, majoring in a variety of fields from art history to animal physiology. Those who had finished school worked in similarly diverse areas, among them education, management, law, health care, and fashion design. Disability often required them to be both flexible and resourceful. "At first I wanted to become a vet," wrote Naomi Passman, "but saw how much lifting was involved and decided against it." Determined to work with animals, she applied to become an apprentice trainer of assistance dogs, but the director of the school turned her down. "I couldn't believe that a person who provided a service for the disabled would not hire me because I *was* disabled!" Undaunted, she found another program. "I am an Apprentice Assistance Dog Trainer and an Independent Living Specialist. I LOVE my work," she reported.

Even though the Americans with Disabilities Act is supposed to prevent the kind of rejection Naomi experienced, a few of the respondents had encountered outright bias, including retaliation by employers if they applied for workers' compensation after being injured on the job. Felicia Wells Williams, with a bachelor's degree in social work, started her career as an entry-level receptionist. "Once after observing blatant discrimination, I filed an equal employment opportunity suit with the Defense Contract Administration/Department of Defense," she recounted. "With the help of some knowledgeable friends, I not only won my case, but I was given the higher grade plus back pay." Defending one's rights can be tricky, however, since the nondisabled tend to expect people with disabilities to be unfailingly cheerful and passive, as Felicia has learned: "Some people say I am arrogant but I believe if I were of normal height/not disabled, I would be called 'confident' rather than 'bossy' or 'pushy.' "

More subtle forms of intolerance can make the workplace a chilly one for disabled women. "Because my symptoms tend to be invisible, I haven't experienced any real bias or discrimination" as a policy advisor to an elected official, reported Cece Hughley Noel, who has had multiple sclerosis since 1987. "However, on the days that I need a cane it is very difficult for me emotionally. People who I work with every day fail to recognize me on the street. They tend to avert their eyes from 'cripples' and don't meet my eyes or hear my 'hello.' It can be devastating to win their praise for taking charge of a meeting one day, only to be ignored as a 'gimp' on the street, the next." Dealing with pain and fatigue every day, Cece has found herself being resented as well as ignored: "My co-workers get 'snitty' sometimes when I take a break and lie down in my office or leave early."

In addition, Cece wrote, "I've used up all my vacation and sick leave this year and feel as though my back is up against the wall." Some of the respondents, finding themselves in similar situations, have had to give up their jobs, and their comments revealed that in our work-driven society, where what you "do" determines who you "are," lack of employment can erode one's sense of self-worth (not to mention one's bank account). As Stephanie McCarty, who managed a bookstore for ten years until her MS symptoms forced her to go on Social Security Disability, put it, "I often feel flustered when I am asked what I 'do' for a living (they wouldn't believe what I do just to live) and don't quite know what to say. I take classes in pottery, spend a great deal of time in the library (and doctor's office), keep myself busy on my home computer, and concentrate on staying healthy. But these things all seem pretty benign when I am talking to someone with a 'career.'"

Whether they held paid jobs or not, these women craved social contact, even at the risk of awkward encounters.

Many recognized that what seems to be rudeness on the part of nondisabled people often arises from ignorance and fear, which can be more crippling in their own way than a physical disability, and that the best way to relieve these is through education. Their advice was pragmatic: Treat a disabled person as an intelligent and responsible adult. (If she's not, that's her problem, not yours.) Remember that not all disabilities are apparent before you accuse her of malingering or shout at her for taking a handicapped parking space. NEVER take one of these yourself, even if you'll "only be a minute." If she does have an obvious disability, before rushing to her aid, ask "How may I help?" and then follow her instructions carefully, or you may both wind up in a heap on the floor. If she's in a wheelchair, sit down whenever possible so that you can converse eye-to-eye, not eye-to-navel. Don't ask her any questions more personal than you'd feel comfortable answering yourself. ("What's wrong with you?" is probably not one of them.) Above all, don't offer her pity. She probably doesn't need it. (And when she does, she can take care of the job herself.)

Many spoke warmly of friends who offer, as one anonymous respondent who was left partially paralyzed by a brain tumor put it, "kindness without condescension." Most of these friends were not disabled, although some of the women still in college reported involvement in disabled students' groups, and most accommodated a disability without much fuss. With both her hearing and her vision impaired, Madeline Cohen has found that "the people who know me best are great about things like repeating themselves, steering me through dark bars and parking lots, and understanding when I miss the thread of a large, noisy conversation and say something ridiculously unconnected. My friends are used to seeing me bump into any object lower than hip level, collide with small children, and look around blankly for someone standing directly in front of me; they do as much as possible to help me avoid such mishaps without making me feel inadequate or foolish."

Sometimes thoughtless friends cause pain without meaning to. Maree Larson, an assistant producer for a video production company who has spina bifida, recalled attending a political rally with some friends, all but one of whom "walked up the steps and took their seats in the third row," while her wheelchair required her to stay in the first. "Soon, my friend was persuaded to join the others ('but only for a minute,' she said), and I was left by myself for the remaining 20 minutes before the rally began." Even friends who are sympathetic in one area can be insensitive in another, as Konie Gardner discovered when it came to dating: "I can't begin to count the number of times that well-meaning friends would say to me, 'I'll set you up with. . . . '" and every time, and I do mean every time, they never once did. I don't think people realize how much a person like me clings to every promise, suggestion, or hint that is made in this regard."

In general, these women found romantic and sexual relationships much more difficult to establish and sustain than simple friendships. A number were troubled by the prevailing social perception of disabled women as incapable of and uninterested in sex: "In this culture people with disabilities are expected to be perpetual children which means that sexual expression would not be appropriate and may be considered perverted," observed Pat Danielson, whose juvenile rheumatoid arthritis was diagnosed when she was four; and twenty-three-year-old Kimberly Mangiafico, who has spinal muscular atrophy, protested that her wheelchair gives most men "the impression that I cannot have sex, which is totally not true. I have a great sexual self-image and I am really comfortable in my own skin." Others recognized internal barriers, like Naomi Passman, who reflected, "I have had boyfriends and even a first love. That part has never been a problem for me; however, when it comes to being sexually involved that's when walls go up. Quite honestly, for me it has not been other people's perceptions that have affected the relationships, it has been my own."

Knowing that they, like nondisabled women, will be judged initially on their appearance, many reported taking great care with their clothes, makeup, and hair. Some were aware of the obvious ironies of this emphasis, like Peggy Merriman, who asked a male friend, "in my most unconcerned and disinterested voice, if he thought any guy would *ever* want to meet or go out with me or even be seen with me, if I was using a wheelchair" and was told, "I don't think it really matters that you're in a wheelchair, because you're so pretty." "Here I was," she went on, "ashamed and embarrassed, because of my physical body. Here he was, praising me and telling me I had nothing to worry about, because of my physical body. He didn't say, 'It doesn't matter, because you are so interesting and intelligent,' or even, 'It doesn't matter, because you have such a cute dog, and anyone who wants to play with him knows you and he are a package deal, unfortunately.' *That* is me; that's who I am."

No matter how pretty or smart a woman may be, or how cute her dog is, "dating and initiating a relationship is difficult though because all of the typical rules never seem to apply when you are in a wheelchair," noted Muffy Davis. "Guys feel that they can really flirt with a girl in a chair but they don't see it as anything serious," since she presumably doesn't expect to be asked out. "Also girls with disabilities can put all the moves on guys and yet the guys will never interpret things the right way." Although she has found that she often has to take the lead, "I really like it when, every once in a while, a guy makes the first move."

Too often, however, he doesn't make any move at all. "I am 27 years old and still a virgin, not that that is bad, but only that it is really not by my choice," wrote Kim Silvey. "I had a date to my prom when I was a junior in high school and went out on a couple of 'just friends' dates in college, but that is it." But disability didn't take away her dreams: "I want nothing more in life than to get married and have a soul-mate, best friend, and lover for life. As each birthday comes and goes, I feel the reality of such happening getting smaller and smaller, and I feel cheated and angry."

Those who had succeeded in establishing relationships often found them complicated, physically and emotionally, by disability. "I worry about what weird noises my body is making that he can hear and I don't," Juli Delzer confided. And a woman who asked to remain anonymous wrote, "Unfortunately, spina bifida did affect my sexual functioning, and I'm not able to achieve orgasm. While we've been able to have a reasonably satisfying sex life without intercourse, I know it bothers my partner that I'm non-orgasmic. I think he sometimes sees it as his failure. I'm very responsive to foreplay with my breasts and around my neck, but am truthfully disappointed myself not to be able to climax." "Due to numbness, weakness, fatigue, and bladder problems we sometimes have to be creative with our lovemaking," noted Stephanie McCarty. A sense of humor also helps: "Often, in the heat of passion, one of my hearing aids will be pressed against a chest, an arm, or a pillow," creating an electronic squeal, wrote Madeline Cohen. "My line, dating back to junior high school: 'Whoops! That's my parents checking up on me.'"

Sometimes the urgency to find a partner contributed to an unwise choice, leading to grief. At twenty-nine, Frances Wallen was paralyzed from the waist down when an 18-wheeler ran a stop sign and struck her red Mazda RX-7. "Before the accident I'd been dating someone fairly seriously," she recalled. "He was wild and unreliable, but I was crazy about him and our affair was very hot. After the accident he was there for me every day and we talked about marriage. I wanted as much of my life back as possible, and figured that this was my last shot at love with someone who could see me without pity. My new husband didn't pity me—he resented me, and took great pleasure in draining me dry financially. I figured he would settle down eventually, but he didn't. We divorced after a year and a half, and I added a broken heart to my list of all my other broken body parts."

But there were happy stories as well. One respondent's husband had abandoned her and their three small children when she was still only mildly disabled by a childhood bout with polio; later, post-polio syndrome caused increasing pain and fatigue, a limp, and breathing problems. At this point, she became friends with a man at the agency where she worked. "He talked to me and we found common ground in our children and love of music," she recollected. "While out in the field I came back to agency headquarters occasionally, and he'd be there, interested in my latest news. When I was moved back on my medical transfer, last year, our friendship grew. I told him, up front, about the polio and the part it played in my life. We married in April 1994. He is there for me, supportive and encouraging and loving. In his eyes I am beautiful, the fact that I have polio doesn't interfere. Through him, I am learning to do my best without exhausting all my energy to 'measure up.' Through him, I've found self-acceptance, self-pride, and love. I look in the mirror and see *normal*."

Fortunately, this experience was far from unique. As Muffy Davis pointed out, "The phone does ring less often, but the guys who do call and are interested are of a higher quality." She's been with one of them for two and a half years now, and many other respondents reported similar good fortune, finding partners who were perceptive, patient, affectionate, and above all reassuring. One respondent, whose brain tumor left her with partial paralysis, as well as hair loss and weight gain, wrote, "Naturally, I don't feel very sexy any more. Yet my husband has continued to treat me with kindness and tenderness. Because of his accepting attitude, my self-esteem has not plummeted entirely." Barbara Maguire, married with two small sons, reflected on her fear that her cerebral pasy might be a burden to her family: "Perhaps my biggest fear is for my husband to someday find out that I am not worth the struggles we've had. He assures me that he is the lucky one and that I am the one 'putting up' with him." "I presently have someone in my life and he is a sweetheart," wrote twenty-five-year-old Stacey Fujii, whose lupus was diagnosed on her twenty-third birthday. "Although he is a surfer, he will do things with me that do not involve the sun, like going out to dinner, to a movie or for a walk on the beach at night. It was very hard for me at first because I felt as if I were holding him back. I was also very insecure about the person I am now, but he always tells me I am beautiful and incredible for what I had to go through. He takes the best care of me and never says I am different, just special."

Not perfect, perhaps, but both normal and special: just the way every women needs to feel. And aided by parents, teachers, friends, lovers, and/or sheer self-determination, the majority of the women who responded had achieved some sense of their own ordinary yet unique qualities. Like Madeline Cohen, they had gained an insight into the human condition which enabled them to see their disabilities as "simply a part of who I am, just as other people have lost parents, gone through divorces, overcome learning disabilities or major illnesses, pulled themselves out of socioeconomic deprivation, or emigrated from war zones." Surely not all would go as far as Kimberly Mangiafico when she wrote that "if I was suddenly given the chance to be able to walk, I would not take it. My being in a wheelchair is part of who I am." But most would understand the self-acceptance her statement implies.

Over all, the women who chose to reveal themselves to *Glamour* were bright, tough, competent, sometimes angry, often funny, and very self-assured—hardly a whiner in the bunch! Theirs were not, as cancer survivor Pat Wallace put it, "triumph-over-tragedy stories" (though there were plenty of tragedies and some triumphs, too) but adventure stories. Stephanie McCarty echoed the sense I often have of exploring uncharted territory: "I feel I have been sent on a journey. I wasn't given a guidebook, so I'll have to draw my own map." In undertaking to live as full human beings in a world intent on reducing them to a set of dysfunctional limbs and organs, they had grown much more vigorous than their sometimes fragile bodies would suggest. As I read and digested their words, I felt honored to count myself among their number.

Getting Byrned

FOR one long afternoon, I commit bigamy, marrying a man I have met only twice before, a marriage of inconvenience, you might say, of necessity. As Wayne and Nancy West, we pull up in front of a modest red-brick ranch house on Tucson's East Side. "This is Warren Cottrell, Arizona Department of Public Safety," he says into a small tape recorder. "It's Wednesday, the eighteenth of July, 1990. With me is Nancy Mairs. We'll be going into 9150 East Kenyon in Tucson, Arizona, to talk to the Byrnes, Joyce and Don Byrne. The time now is 10:52 and we've started the tape recorder." After burying the machine in the bottom of my large canvas handbag, he retrieves my manual wheelchair from the trunk, sets it up, and settles me into it for the slog up the gravel drive to the front door.

I have only the haziest idea of what we're in for. I have

never been—either by profession or in fantasy—an undercover agent, and until a couple of weeks ago, I didn't even know that an ordinary person could become one. Then Warren, together with Barbara Gelband, a lawyer who prosecutes organized crime and racketeering in the Arizona attorney general's office, approached me at the recommendation of another lawyer there, who has long been a personal friend. They had begun to receive complaints from people in the Tucson area about Byrne Viral International, a company marketing a remedy for a spectrum of illnesses, among them multiple sclerosis. Chronically ill, sometimes incapacitated, these people had each paid some thousands of dollars, often exhausting life savings or borrowing heavily from relatives, for a series of treatments, administered intravenously and by subcutaneous injections of "advanced, fast-acting pharmaceuticals, with no known side effects." When they failed to improve, or even felt worse, a few became skeptical enough to alert the attorney general.

This was not the first time Byrne Viral International had attracted attention. In fact, in the Phoenix area a couple of years earlier a pair of investigators from the attorney general's office, responding to complaints, had attempted to gather evidence that the Byrnes—neither of them an M.D.—were practicing medicine without a license, but Don and Joyce became suspicious and refused to deal with them. Warier but undaunted, the Byrnes shifted their venue a hundred miles or so south. What they needed, Warren and Barbara told me, was someone genuinely ill, who could realistically receive the Byrnes' pitch, a recording of which, they hoped, would provide the grounds for a search warrant. They had been reluctant to enlist my aid lest I too succumb to the Byrnes' blandishments—the last thing they wanted was to create yet another victim—but my friend Noreen had said, "You don't know Nancy. You'd better meet her and read her work before you decide."

I like to be thought of as a tough customer. I was a little startled, then, when George and I both felt the allure of the videotape Barbara lent us. Professionally created and smoothly narrated by the husband of a Byrne client, it stopped well short of promising a cure while holding out hope for improvement: increased energy and strength, perhaps even the chance to walk again. We found ourselves wondering whether maybe, just maybe. . . . Forewarned, we weren't in true jeopardy, but we could well imagine why a person, after years of suffering unalleviated by conventional medicine, might leap at such bait. Since I understood such vulnerability from the inside, watching the way the slick video exploited fear and exhaustion and despair made me angry. It's that anger that fuels my determination to be a true trouper as Warren bumps me up the front step and presses the doorbell.

The dark-haired woman who answers our ring identifies herself as Joyce. "Don's in here," she says, leading us into the front room. This would seem cramped even without the large wheelchair in the middle, in which a tall, balding man is propped, his ventilator clicking and purring beneath him. He has amyotrophic lateral sclerosis, commonly called ALS or Lou Gehrig's disease—I know from the flyer put out by Byrne Viral—diagnosed when he was twenty-six. Now about fifty-five, he owes his longevity to treatment with "anti-viral pharmaceuticals," he claims. It is true that most people don't survive ALS for very long (though the astrophysicist Stephen Hawking is one notable exception), so this man is remarkable; even so, I find it hard to believe that he is currently "rehabilitating" his diaphram to breathe without assistance and even learning to walk again. I've seldom seen anyone who looked less robust. My heart shudders with pity adulterated by the dread—never far beneath my surface serenity—that my MS, a particularly severe form, will one day bring me to a similar pass.

Poor heart, it's already floundering with a different sort of trepidation. In the guise of Nancy West, I am here to trick this ruin of a man and his wife, and I am not sure I can pull it off. As anyone who has read my books knows (and we hope that the Byrnes have not), I am a lousy dissembler. This is not merely a character defect (though some people, elderly relatives in particular, believe it to be that) but a matter of principle. Now, for the sake of the justice Barbara and Warren have convinced me must be served, I have contracted to break my years-long vow not to tell lies, no matter how convenient, a vow I have kept with some rigor. Today my success depends upon prevarication.

I plunge right in. "This is a nice house," I comment

brightly, though it's not a nice house at all—it's pokey and ill-furnished and stifling despite a noisy fan—but Joyce has disappeared without explanation, and on a ventilator Don can't speak, and if I don't say something to fill up the silence I'll jump straight out of my skin. Fortunately, Joyce rematerializes, and there commences the queerest conversation I have ever participated in, Don's lips silently stretching and pursing, fishlike, Joyce translating these grimaces into strings of words. Occasionally she falters and begins to utter individual letters, as though he were spelling: "There's a b-a-t—be—bad spot on one eye . . . ." Is she merely doing this for effect, to persuade us that she's lipreading what is actually a carefully rehearsed routine? Is Don really "speaking," directing the conversation as he appears to do, or—a more sinister thought—is he a pawn of this woman and their sons, forced by his helplessness to carry out this charade for their gain?

This bizarre entity Don/Joyce questions me at some length about my symptoms. Because I've been trained as a symptomatic patient instructor, teaching medical students how to give neurological exams, I have a fair amount of technical knowledge about my condition, which I'm not supposed to betray. I carry the process of dumbing myself down a little far. Asked how long I've been using a wheelchair, I say, "Uh, I started to use it part time about ten years ago, but, uh, only in the last couple of years have I used it a lot. I still don't use it at home, you know, in the house, uh, I walk around, but I don't—I—I get so tired now that I don't have the energy like, you know, to go into a store and walk around long enough to do my shopping and stuff, so I use it mainly because of that." To my own ears, I sound like Moon Zappa's Valley Girl, but no one else seems to find my burbling peculiar.

After instructing me to stand up and sit back down several times, Don/Joyce poses a series of questions in no discernible order: Do I wake up as tired as when I went to bed? Do my ankles swell? Has my skin ever been yellow? Do I get headaches? When did my symptoms start? When did I have my children? Do I have joint pain? Have my shoulder blades atrophied? Are my palms red? Where did I grow up? Do I get up in the night to urinate? On the basis of my answers, a bombshell: I DON'T HAVE MULTIPLE SCLEROSIS AFTER ALL. "The reason that it was s—so s-l—slow for you to get a diagnosis was that it is probably the wrong diagnosis," Don/Joyce explains. "You do not have the classic symptoms of MS," which would include "shaking so much you would have to have a lap cloth to tie you into the chair," as well as urination every hour during the night and vision so blurred "you should not be able to see my face," but not the fatigue that has been my most persistent bugbear. "It is probably a d-e—disease that is also a virus, that is called polymyositis."

I don't have to act dumbstruck. I really am. "But—but can you treat people with this condition?" I ask, fearful that we'll get turned away without what we came for.

"We have—we probably have more patients with polymyositis than we do actual MS patients. The difference is that the rehabilitation is better, a lot shorter than with MS." Oh good, I'm still in the running. In addition to my symptoms, however, I need a blood test to confirm the diagnosis before they will discuss treatment. Yikes! Warren and Barbara said emphatically that I was to undergo no medical procedures as part of this operation. Does a blood test count? "All it is is a little pinprick and he gets a few little drops of blood off you," Joyce reassures me, referring to Juan, the young man who has just come in and been introduced variously as their chauffeur and "the manager of our facilities in Mexico."

Warren and I can hardly adjourn for a little undercover conference, and it's clear that we'll miss the rest of the pitch without the blood test. With a glance at him, I say as firmly as I can, "I don't mind." Actually, I do mind something wicked. For some reason, I've always had a horror of getting blood drawn from my finger. You can drain it from my arm by the bucket, but even the tale of Sleeping Beauty pricking her finger on a spindle gives me the collywobbles.

"It's entirely up to you," Warren says neutrally. "It's your finger." As he pushes me into the next room where the procedure is to be carried out, however, he asks quietly, "You sure you want to do this?"

"I'm sure. I'm sure. I just hate having my finger pricked." Fearful of fainting, I concentrate on Juan as he takes out a sterile lancet and wipes my finger with an alcohol swab, then look away before the stab. Still conscious, I stare at the television screen in the corner, where curious figures are now swimming erratically: my blood cells blown up about three thousand times. Juan takes Polaroid snapshots of them while Don/Joyce explains that my liver isn't metabolizing protein properly and my blood is full of toxins indicative of an infection, undoubtedly polymyositis.

"Is there a standard treatment for it then that we could get from an M.D.?" Warren asks.

"No," says Don/Joyce, "I have developed the only antiviral pharmaceuticals that can treat it. I was the first person that had ever been successfully treated for ALS and I developed the pharmaceuticals to treat the other viruses. We treat ALS, MS, Parkinson's, lupus, MD with defective tissue, and polymyositis. Okay. We can go in the other room and we will talk about the treatment."

At last! We've been here well over an hour. Warren has already excused himself to use the bathroom, taking my bag along in order to flip the tape, an awkward maneuver but no one seemed disturbed by it. The closeness and heat have increased my weakness, and I'm exhausted, both from the effort of sustaining my golly-gee-whiz persona, so antithetical to my usual wryness, and from the struggle to make sense of Don/Joyce's chaotic and evasive presentation. I just want to go home and suffer my MS in peace.

I "probably" have polymyositis. They have "a lot of patients with this," responding well to treatment. I will have to go back and forth to Nogales, about seventy-five miles south of Tucson, because their licenses are all in

Mexico; there a doctor at their clinic will do further blood tests and then start me on medication, "light" doses to begin with, to get me ready for the "heavy treatment." These treatments, lasting about four weeks, are administered intravenously. Thereafter, every day I will give myself an "arm shot" and a "rib shot," using a "very tiny needle," and also take several "tablets" or "capsules."

No side effects will occur "except for sore arms for a few weeks while your body is building up antibodies, but this medication has the ability to rebuild the myelin sheath" using proteins "very similar to the proteins in your own body." Don himself has taken one of the shots more than twelve hundred times; Joyce takes one for arthritis every day; even their children and grandchildren take boosters to build their immune systems, since "all these pharmaceuticals have the ability for your body to build its own interferon." An irony here, hidden from me for now: in almost exactly a year, my husband—the real one—will begin to give himself daily subcutaneous injections of legitimate alpha-interferon in an attempt to enhance his immune system against metastatic melanoma.

"Do you have brochures on the different types of medicine?" Warren asks.

"We do not. We do not." Nothing in writing.

"How much does a thing like this cost?"

"Between $7,500 and $9,500." Whew! This is considerably more than most of the others have reported paying. We look pretty affluent, I suppose. I have dressed casually but carefully in a cream-colored knit top from Talbots and a pale green skirt from a fancy shop at the edge of the Dartmouth campus, and you can't tell just by looking that they both came from end-of-season sales racks during last summer's trip to New England. Warren's car, visible from the window behind me, is a large white Buick, relatively new, confiscated in a drug bust, could he possibly have told me, or is my under-cover imagination running away with me? I suppose we've been sized up as a pair of prosperous burghers and hit up accordingly. This price is for the first six months; in the second six, the cost goes down to eight or nine hundred, perhaps even less thereafter. The treatments will continue for "probably two years." We can seek re-imbursement from Blue Cross if we wish, but insurance is "not something we get involved in at all," Joyce says dismissively.

I feel a curious attraction toward this course of treat-ment I know full well has no effect but to augment the Byrnes' income while depleting mine, the same sort of tug George and I felt a couple of nights earlier while watching the promotional video. In recent years, my de-terioration has speeded up alarmingly; though I don't know it, in a couple of weeks a fall on my head will con-sign me to a scooter, and then a wheelchair, forever. I would give plenty just to stop this process, and even more to reverse it. Although not truly in danger of plunking down several thousand dollars and booking my first trip to a Mexican clinic, I can understand oth-ers' doing so.

Having asked all the questions we decently can, we make our good-byes, promising to let the Byrnes know our decision within the next few days. Do they believe us? I wonder. Are they already planning how to spend our money as we drive away? In the car, Warren is elated. He feels confident that we have enough material to justify a search warrant, and sure enough, the next afternoon, he telephones to say he has secured one and his team will go in first thing in the morning.

That evening brings a funny little coda to the previous day's adventure. George and I are watching television at the back of the house when the front doorbell rings. It's Juan the chauffeur-cum-blood-technician, delivering some xeroxed information about polymyositis, my new disease.

"This is for Nancy West," Juan says, holding the packet out to George.

"Huh?" After twenty-seven years, George has grown so accustomed to thinking of me as his wife that he forgets I belong to somebody else now, too.

"This is for Nancy West," Juan repeats. "Is she here?"

"Oh, Nancy *West*. Yes, she's here. I'll give it to her. Thanks."

He returns to the family room, laughing but a little worried. We can only hope that Juan, assuming that George simply had trouble understanding his accent, hasn't raced back to his employers to say there was something fishy about Nancy West. Otherwise, Warren may arrive in the morning to find that his Byrnes have once again flown.

/ / /

When this scenario had played out to its desired end—when Warren called me the next day to say that the operation had gone smoothly, his team seizing papers, the equipment used for blood tests, and boxes of chemicals stored in the garage—I was oddly cast down. I had considered the whole undertaking, insofar as it involved me, as a kind of caper, a novel experience I'd better grab when it offered itself. After all, how many people ever get the chance to go undercover? I hadn't anticipated any emotional response, certainly not this one: sadness melded with something like remorse. I thought of Don and Joyce's dismay when Warren returned to their door waving a search warrant. It seemed a violation of hospitality in which, they were sure to realize, I had connived. Never mind that they'd been more than willing to fleece me while I sojourned under their roof. I had still entered under false pretenses, and I was embarrassed.

My compunction passed before long, and the entire episode slid toward the back of my cluttered consciousness like a novelty gift that, though you have no earthly use for it, seems too clever to be shoved into the dustbin. I had no special stake in the case. Had I been a criminal, I suppose I might have bartered my services for a reduced sentence or even a whole new identity; but MS lasts for life, without reprieve, certainly without the possibility of shucking off a cripple's character to become some other person. My mother wanted me to reap fame and fortune from the affair because, like any good mother, she believes her offspring entitled to fame and fortune for every harebrained scheme they undertake. I had volunteered my services on condition of anonymity, however, terms unconducive to wealth and renown, though my anonymity became moot when a local newspaper reporting the case referred to me as "a well-known Tucson author with multiple sclerosis," thereby narrowing the list of suspects pretty dramatically. As it was, I earned no more than a letter from the attorney general of the State of Arizona thanking me for being a good citizen.

I knew, of course, that I might be required to testify if the investigation led to charges against the Byrnes, but legal wheels grind so slowly that this seemed hardly inevitable. Not until more than two years later was I called as a witness at a hearing to determine whether adequate evidence existed to bring them to trial on the charge of practicing medicine without a license. By then, Warren had retired and Barbara had taken another position, turning the case over to two other attorneys, John Davis and Sylvia Goodwin. Before the hearing, they brought me the tapes, together with a transcript, of my conversation with the Byrnes, but although I was thus armed with the facts, once again I found myself ill-prepared for my emotional response.

For one thing, I had to face Don and Joyce, whom I hadn't seen since they closed their door behind me, believing, I had hoped, that some thousands of my money would soon fatten their wallets. They must despise me for my duplicity. I might have eased my chagrin if I could have reduced them purely to a pair of larcenous and remoseless scoundrels—"true sociopathic personalities" in Sylvia's words—as very likely they were. But there sat Don, former meatcutter and self-styled bio-chemical researcher, gaunt and feeble, a crocheted afghan over his legs, his ventilator whooshing rhythmically. Could he really be a "tyrant" to his workers, as one of his victims would later characterize him to me? What force could he exert? Was Joyce truly the compliant Mormon wife, or might she, his sisters, and his five sons really have conspired to exploit his condition for their own gain, forcing him to display himself and wiggle his lips on cue or else, when they were alone, they would refuse to feed and clothe and clean him, the unspoken possibility that had pierced my cripple's heart with horror? Perhaps they both have genuinely believed all along that the bottles of "pharmaceuticals" (containing, a confidential informant told investigators, "amino acetose" obtained from a local chiropractor, the labels removed, though the mixture proved too unstable for reliable chemical analysis) held the secret to Don's remarkable survival and that "there are patients all over the world who are dying because they cannot get these pharmaceuticals," as they told *Tucson Citizen* reporter Carla McClain when she made the investigation public. How should I know? I could be certain only that the human issues were more complicated than they appeared.

My distress was aggravated by the adversarial and reductive nature of court proceedings. Squeezed at an awkward angle into a space whose architect clearly had never envisioned wheelchairs, I swore to "tell" the truth, something I have no idea how to do. Although I know how to search for the truth, even to suggest the truth, I don't believe in it, as the law does, as a discrete entity—like a trinket in a Christmas pudding—which can be isolated and plunked down with an "aha!" As John Davis questioned me, the defense attorney, Charles Thomas, kept leaping up to object to my ruminative rhetorical style. At one point, when he complained, "It's a speculation," right in the middle of my sentence, I completed my thought, forcing the judge's stern reproof: "When the attorney stands up and makes an objection, you need to stop talking so that we can deal with the legalities." Clearly my grandmother's rules of etiquette did not apply here.

Most troublesome, amidst all this truth-telling, there seemed to be no room for moral reflection. Mr. Thomas's defense appeared to be that the Byrnes were merely conducting research, using their profits to support scientific facilities in Mexico; they were not practicing medicine, since they never offered to treat me themselves (this being done by the doctors at a "clinic," a couple of barren rooms, in Nogales, Sonora) or to cure my "probable" polymyositis. And indeed, in the dozens of times I have reviewed the transcript, I can see how careful they were to avoid such promises, using the vaguest and most conditional phrasing. They might say, "We have people that were dragging a foot and one arm was gone and they couldn't grip anything and they've come back all the way"; but if I were fool enough to infer in my desperation that I, with my foot-drop and paralyzed left arm and weak grasp, could also fully recover, that was my problem, not theirs. I had no opportunity to object that leading people who suffer the anxiety and pain and muddled thinking that accompany illness to false conclusions, however indirectly, though it might be legally acceptable, was morally reprehensible. The "law" had no interest in my moral squeamishness.

Although John and Sylvia seemed pleased by the proceedings, I left the courtroom dispirited. Some experiences, I've learned painfully, are not worth having: appearing on the Oprah Winfrey Show was one; busting a quack might turn out to be another. Still, I was committed now; if the case did come to trial, I would have to testify again. *If.*

Years passed. Joyce had been indicted but not yet brought to trial, and after the Byrnes set up operations again in Nogales, Arizona, in 1992, Don was indicted as well for conspiracy to commit fraud and conspiracy to practice medicine without a license. Returning to the Phoenix suburb of Mesa, where the investigation had originally begun in 1988, they continued their activities despite the indictments, all the while receiving one postponement of the trial after another, of which I was duly informed by the Victim Rights and Witness Assistance office.

Because Don was "not competent based on the fact that he cannot assist his attorney in his defense," for nearly two years attempts were made to obtain equipment on which he could be trained to communicate without Joyce's interpretation. During this period, Charles Thomas withdrew from the case and new attorneys had to be appointed, a transition that caused further delay. Finally, on March 20, 1995, the court, determining that a communication system would be "prohibitively expensive," ordered the indictment against Don dismissed. John and Sylvia then proceeded quickly toward Joyce's trial. On April 25, I received a criminal subpoena ordering me to appear on May 2. Even though I was expecting it, this unnerved me, especially the line reading, "IF YOU FAIL TO APPEAR AS ORDERED, A WARRANT MAY BE ISSUED FOR YOUR ARREST." To hell with moral qualms: I was *dying* to go to court again.

In the end, I was reprieved by a "non-trial disposition." Pleading guilty, Joyce was sentenced to three years' probation and ordered to pay restitution of $60,551. This amount nowhere near represented their earnings from the scam—they apparently took in $170,000 in the first six months of 1990 alone—but at least the nine victims named in the suit might get back their payments, ranging from $5,000 to $9,500 apiece. Such a resolution, if not exactly satisfactory, came as a relief. No one had wanted either Don, a complete invalid, or Joyce, his primary caregiver, sent to prison. The objective of the whole dragged-out affair had been to halt their operation, which would in fact be difficult to continue as long as Joyce remained on probation. No one I spoke to seemed to feel any doubt that, as soon as probation ended, they'd go right back to their old tricks.

Later, I was permitted to look at some of the records, which afforded me glimpses into a tale that might have been composed by Kafka crossed with Lewis Carroll. The guest room at the back of the Tucson house filled with chairs and beds, people sitting or reclining on them, sticking needles into each other's veins, IVs dangling from curtain rods or taped to walls; one son's estranged lover, telling the prosecutors how he helped "cook up" the pharmaceuticals; the young Canadian with MS, whose father had sold the family farm to raise the $10,000 for his treatment, holding his infant son in his IV-bruised arms after he'd returned from the clinic in Mexico; the young woman in Nogales, hired to type and edit Don's "book," sitting for hours in front of a green screen glowing with amber letters while Don, propped in his hospital bed, watched over her shoulder and made a "noiselike whisper" at every typing error. Joyce told the typist-editor they had a treatment that could "clear up" her epilepsy. After a few days, she had gathered enough from her reading, observations, and talk with the various people milling in and out to suspect that something bad was going on; and, uncomfortable with her own involvement, she telephoned the attorney general's office. "Strange, just the whole atmosphere there," she concluded her deposition. "It was just weird. It was just weird."

Invited to attend the sentencing, I had the chance at last to meet six of the victims named in the case; and at my request, made through Victim Rights and Witness Assistance, four of them agreed to speak to me afterward by telephone about their experiences. I was struck, despite their obvious differences in age, sex, and circumstance, by some of their commonalities. For one thing, among them they reported an overlapping array of conditions—asthma, blood problems, adrenal exhaustion, allergies, environmental illness, chronic fatigue syndrome, candida, arthritis, back pain, emphysema, migraine—which rely heavily on subjective reporting for diagnosis and, once diagnosed, resist or defy treatment. I do not mean to dismiss their complaints as "all in their heads" (and anyway, even neurotic pain hurts) but to point out that conventional doctors are apt to be skeptical of conditions that don't show up unequivocally on tests and discouraged by the failure of patients to respond to medications. Then the *doctors* become dismissive. All the victims reported seeking medical relief for years, to no avail. No wonder they were susceptible to the attentions of people who seemed not just willing but eager to treat them and confident of the benefits.

In addition, all were essentially alone—two single, one widowed, the fourth married to a nonsupportive husband. They were even isolated. Ellen, for instance, has lived by herself since her husband died in 1977 and doesn't drive, so she is pretty well stuck in a retirement community south of Tucson which lacks public transportation. The program offered a clear social element: victims might travel together to Mexico in the Byrnes' van or, after learning to give IVs to each other, gather in their home for treatments. Susan felt that the Byrnes treated her with love, as though she were part of their family, so that even after she realized that she felt worse rather than better, she found it hard to break away. Becky, too, mentioned that the Byrnes were good at "bonding," creating a family feeling; she "practically lived" at their house, where people from all over the world with all kinds of diseases made the atmosphere interesting and "crazy." In a life cramped by pain and the perception that the world is a stew of substances that will make one ill, the opportunity for social contact with sympathetic others must strengthen a regimen's appeal.

No one got better. Blase experienced no change at all; Becky felt better only briefly and, she thinks now, coincidentally; Ellen and Susan developed such abdominal discomfort and bloating that they quit. By the same token, apparently no one was physically harmed. It is hard to ascertain how many victims (and there were at least dozens of them, maybe more) delayed or forwent useful therapy while under the Byrnes' care or will do so in the future because they've grown wary of all practitioners. Becky, for instance, in 1991 finally went to a chronic-pain specialist who medicated her for pain and insomnia, and since then her condition has improved. Psychological damage is even harder to gauge. Blase blames himself for what happened. Ellen, who felt anger at first but then relief to have the episode behind her, is still ashamed of herself. Susan believes she's lost her credibility, because she referred others to the Byrnes, and feels "brainwashed." Becky's fury is directed at the medical and legal establishments, who ignored or "used" her, rather than at Don, for whom she almost "roots" as just one crook among many. "At least the guy was trying," she says, and he outsmarted everyone.

About the financial damage there's no question. These people were not wealthy to begin with. Blase spent $6,000, and when he requested a refund, the Byrnes refused. Becky paid them $5,000. Ellen paid $4,000, quitting when they asked her for another $1,000. When the Byrnes offered to make a "new person" of Susan for $6,000, she borrowed the money from an elderly aunt; they offered to pay her for the referrals she gave them but never did. None of them is likely to see the money again. So far, Blase, Susan, and Becky have each received $13 and Ellen $10.11. The Byrnes appear to have a genius for hiding their assets, and Joyce claims to be unable to afford to pay restitution. The attorney general's office is seeking forfeiture of some of their property, and Joyce has now been ordered to pay $100 per month. Since this must be divided nine ways, clearly no one is going to live long enough to recoup the full amount owed.

Like Ellen, I feel relieved to have the case behind me. I am not unmarked by the experience, however. It has left me even more cynical than I was before. I signed on believing that I could serve the cause of justice. Now I feel certain that justice does not exist, not in any systemic sense. Bad actions are as likely to be permitted as punished. People who have been hurt may well be hurt more. That which happens—*wyrd*, the Anglo-Saxons called it—is intrinsically arbitrary and beyond human control. The only means for living with the way the world is, and the way people are in it, are resignation and forgiveness: to accept the Byrnes' greed, their victims' gullibility, my own moral shilly-shally, the legal system's sluggishness and ineptitude, life's incessant, infernal whimsy. Justice may or may not get done. Right action can't depend on an entity so capricious. We shall have to find our satisfaction elsewhere.

And in an odd way, satisfaction serves as the crux of this whole tale, its lack the motivating force. God knows it's hard to come by in the best of circumstances, and nobody here was in circumstances worth a hoot. Clearly the Byrnes weren't content with their lives. I don't suppose criminals ever are. If they didn't believe in their pharmaceuticals, they were greedy for profits. If they did, they were driven by something darker, a horror of Don's condition, a failure to come to terms with its incurability, a dread of death. That their victims were similarly driven equipped them singularly well for the task of seduction: they knew only too well what to offer. The victims, seeking to escape unbearable limitations, leaped at the vaguest promises, eager to subject their bodies to anything for relief.

To the nondisabled, despondency and desperation may seem the natural, indeed the necessary, response to pain, fatigue, and debility: it seems so unquestionably awful being who we are that we must naturally seek to cease being who we are at any price. But as a woman who now qualifies to number herself among the severely disabled, I dare say not merely that they are wrong but that this attitude contributes to neglect of the needs of people with disabilities. After all, if you believe we're *supposed* to be miserable, why should you undertake to alleviate our misery? Despondency and desperation signal distress and require remedy in anyone, however, regardless of physical condition. Disabled people with adequate physical and emotional support, proper medication for pain and depression, and ample activity that seems meaningful to them do not—and ought not—take less pleasure in their lives than anyone else. And people who find their lives fulfilling are unlikely to go running after charlatans who promise to turn those lives into something else.

I don't repudiate alternatives to conventional medicine. I receive massage therapy and use a neuromuscular stimulator regularly, and I take so many dietary supplements that I undoubtedly produce the most expensive pee in Tucson. I am also married to a man who is surviving melanoma for reasons no one fully understands. Perhaps the surgeon really did scrape every malignant cell out of the abdominal wall into which the tumor had grown, or the concoction of toxic chemicals he received eighteen times killed off any strays without killing him first. Maybe the tamoxifen he swallowed for five years starved the cells, or the interferon he injected for four enabled his immune system to fight them off. But what has been the role of the carrots he's eaten or the meditation he's engaged in daily? What about the fact that he was the only person to whom it never occurred that he was going to die? I'm not going to dismiss any of these elements. But neither of us is about to engage in any financially or physiologically

risky behaviors. Our lives are too precious and de-
lightful to us as they are, even though they include MS
and cancer (and migraines and impotence and hay fever
and heat rash every summer).

The onus for ensuring that a person with even serious
limitations can lead a satisfactory life doesn't fall entirely on the nondisabled, of course, although the re-
moval of architectural and other environmental barriers, together with the provision of affordable equipment
and services, essential for active engagement in the
world requires at least their collaboration. Most of the
work of living well and fully in the teeth of pain and uncertainty, as well as social neglect or ostracism, falls
squarely on the disabled person herself, challenged by
circumstance to come to terms with the knowledge
that her condition will never improve, that it will probably get worse, and that it may even cause her to die: not
a cheery scenario, but one not vastly different from that
facing every other creature. I imagine a world where
people, allowed the space to accept—admit, endure,
embrace—their diverse and often difficult realities,
will be able to take reasonable measures to ensure basic
health without getting burned by a doctor eager to in-
ject them with cobra venom, a dentist willing to tear
out all their dental work, or a butcher-turned-
biochemist who wants to drip clear fluids from unla-
beled bottles into their veins.

Then this undercover agent will be, only too gladly,
out of a job.

Writing West:
A Reclamation Project

IN SEVENTH or eighth grade I first undertook to write about the West. I don't still have that manuscript, but since I didn't own a typewriter in those days, it must have been written in my round italic hand, probably in pencil on the lined paper we were issued for school assignments, in time stolen from those assignments. Already touchy about my family's ambivalence toward my literary pretensions, I would have worked in secret, in my room papered with pink and white gladioli at the front of our shingled Cape Cod, grey with Nantucket blue shutters, outside the village I have come to call Enon, though that hasn't been its name in something like three hundred years.

The work was a novel, commissioned by my friend Sal. She lived just down the road, in a white colonial at the side of a little pond, but every summer her divorced mother would take her and her younger brother out to Jackson Hole, Wyoming, which she plainly felt was her true home. A lanky girl, redheaded and freckled, who hated getting her period and wearing dresses to school and going to parties and all the other impositions that were making ladies of us, she would come back each fall listless and melancholy. Then, at the end of one summer, she came back smitten. He was a cowboy named Peter, years and years older than we, at least eighteen, maybe even twenty, too old to know she existed anyway, but she was crazy about him. To make up for his disregard, and the horrible distance that now lay between them, Sal asked me to write about the love she hoped they would share one day.

Obviously the story must be set in Wyoming, since cattle ranches in New England are few and far between, and anyway Sal was heading out there for good as soon as she gained her independence (as I believe she did). I wasn't awfully well prepared for the task. I watched *The Lone Ranger* faithfully every Saturday, over a lunch of cream of mushroom soup and Waverly Wafers, but on the whole snowy crags and drawling men in chaps seemed more exotic to me than palm-fringed beaches and brown-skinned women picking mangoes, since I had actually once lived in the South Pacific. Fortunately, Sal had a few snapshots and a memory made vivid by longing. I never have seen the Grand Tetons, only Wyoming's endless wind-scoured southern plains, yet I still carry in my head the images of them Sal stamped there nearly forty years ago.

The only details of my novel I can recall have to do with lots of passionate kissing (but nothing else, since what else did I know?) in a sleeping bag beside a campfire on an icy night under a blaze of stars. Coming up with these can't have overtaxed my imagination, bolstered as it was by games of post office and sleep-outs at summer camp. Sal greeted each new installment with gratifying avidity, and I must have produced about seventy pages before we lost interest in the project. I wonder if she ever forgot Peter, though. I wish I could find and ask her.

I never dreamed then, or for years and years afterward, that I would move west myself. Where I come from, Chicago is "west," and I never even thought of going there. My impressions of the West remained vague and mostly antiquated, gleaned during high school from TV westerns like *Gunsmoke*, *Maverick*, and *Have Gun*, *Will Travel*. Except for *McCabe and Mrs. Miller* much later, I didn't care for western films. And aside from *The Virginian* and *Giants in the Earth*, which were assigned in school, and *Ramona*, which I devoured repeatedly on my own, I avoided western novels. Majoring in English literature at a liberal arts college did nothing to correct my bias. "O western wind, when wilt thou blow?" definitely did not allude to a chinook.

Just after college graduation, I drove with friends to Chicago and far, far beyond, along Route 66 all the way to southern New Mexico, and during my couple of weeks there I was so enchanted by the vastness and intensity of the sky and by the ceaseless play of light on the Organ Mountains that I contemplated moving to the desert someday. But "someday" is an almost infinite span to twenty-year-olds, and as I moved to Rhode Island, then to Maine, and finally back to Massachusetts, the desert in memory came to seem almost as unreal as it had done before my brief sojourn there.

When, less than ten years later, desperate for warmth and light, I migrated westward, husband and children in tow, to a place where people refer to Chicago as the East, to hear some of our family and friends you'd have thought we were about to drop off the edge of the earth. On my father's side, my family has lived in New England for some fourteen generations. My mother's side contains some newcomers, but no one more recent than my great-grandparents, and once they got settled they remained within a twenty-five-mile radius of Boston. To Bostonians, this city really is the hub of the universe, a perception I have never quite been able to shake myself, and the desire to go elsewhere suggests a certain instability, mental or moral or, in the most serious cases, both.

All the same, I came to Tucson, where I have remained for more than two decades. Tucson lies in the West. Here I've become a writer, and because my work draws upon personal experience, Tucson provides the setting for much of it. For a couple of years, I directed the Western States Project on Women in the Curriculum. A volume of my poems won the Western States Book Award. I'm listed in *Who's Who in the West*. Still, I have never presumed to identify myself as a western writer, and I don't know that anyone else would call me one either.

Who *would* I put into this class? Certainly Edward Abbey, his Pennsylvania origins wholly eclipsed by his passion both for the West's pure open spaces and for the right of the individual to protect them by any means from rapacious governmental and commercial forces. Charles Bowden, Abbey's avatar though not his imitator, documenting the spoliation that individuals have proved helpless to prevent. Richard Shelton, the Sonoran desert's own poet, and James Griffith, its chronicler. I've deliberately chosen residents of Tucson, who sometimes write (though seldom kindly) about the city, to suggest that my choice of residence alone does not disqualify me.

They are all men, and so perhaps the problem is my gender. But no, women have long been regarded as western writers. Think of the diaries and letters historians have mined for details to authenticate their portrayal of pioneer experience. Think of Mary Austin, and later Willa Cather, and Eva Antonia Wilbur-Cruce later still. Think of some of the most captivating work now being produced in the region: Linda Hasselstrom's delineation of life on a Montana ranch; Terry Tempest Williams's weaving of human mortality into the natural world's wide web; Kathleen Norris's contemplation of community and solitude on the Dakota plains. Gender bias has not silenced the voices of these women. But although I am every bit the woman they are, I am still not a western writer.

I am hardly alone in my exclusion. In fact, I suspect that if we took a census, the majority of writers living in the West would wind up out here in the cold with me. Terry McMillan set *Waiting to Exhale* in Phoenix, but no one would ever call her a western writer. No more would they call Armistead Maupin one, though his novels take place in San Francisco, which is almost as far west as you can get and still be in the territory where the term "western writer" was coined. True, the action in these occurs in cities, but an urban setting isn't an automatic disqualifier, as the title of Rudolfo Anaya's most recent novel—*Albuquerque*—makes plain. Some other restrictive rule is at work.

I am neither African American nor gay, and I don't know enough about the experiences specific to ethnic or sexual difference to speculate on the reasons for excluding them from the literature of the West. But I know a whole hell of a lot about difference based on physical disability; and I can tell you that to be a western writer, as that term is conventionally understood, you gotta have legs. I mean working—hard-working—ones. I have a pair, which are cosmetically serviceable, I suppose, but they're not much good for anything else. Certainly not for gripping the flanks of a horse as I ride out through a spring blizzard to check on newborn calves, nor for tramping the margins of Great Salt Lake as it inundates the habitat of coots and curlews, not even for standing beneath a clothesline, bending and sorting and pinning my laundry in the sweetening sun and wind.

My crippled life began when I moved from Boston to Tucson. This pure coincidence split my history: there was once a whole youthful Nancy, who grew up in a gentle geography though a severe climate; then there was an aging Nancy, who limped and later stumbled and finally stopped walking altogether, in a milder climate but a formidable geography. Young, I ambled through New England's variegated terrain—bridle path, beach, brook—in all weathers with authentic, though largely sentimental, affection for the natural world, which seemed to me compassable and therefore hospitable. I have lived now for more than twenty years in a landscape too large for me, and getting larger as my physical condition deteriorates, the conventional West—land, lots of land, 'neath the starry skies above— and the conventional responses to it—exploration, exploitation—demanding a physical vigor I've never enjoyed here.

Above all, the West is expansive: beneath an immense translucent hemisphere, sere plains stretching to snow-crowned ranges and beyond them the sweep of the earth's greatest ocean, a geography so overwhelmingly empty, even today, as to make one long to be everywhere at once. The terrain itself may account for the "rootlessness, mobility, and rugged individualism" that, in the common view, continue to characterize "western experience,"[1] a classic formulation I came across just in this week's reading. Although rootlessness and rugged individualism seem to possess less value for the women than the men writing today, every-one appears to agree upon mobility. A recent newspaper article has this: "Out here, you can still drive fast. The forerunner of driving fast was riding fast. Thus, the American condition: wandering. The urge to saddle your car and move quickly through time and space has resulted in that ancient national ritual, the road trip, and the sacred texts that have accompanied it."[2] On your feet, on your horse, in your car, movement's the thing.

I am, as one particularly unfortunate (circum)locu-tion would have it, mobility-impaired. I don't walk, I don't canter, I don't drive. I roll. Seated in a frame of black-painted aluminum with twelve-inch wheels in the back and eight-inch wheels in the front, steering with a joystick, under ideal conditions I can do 4.9 miles an hour around my neighborhood. If I want to go faster or farther, I roll onto a platform that, with the flip of a couple of switches, deposits me wheelchair and all in the back of my van, where whoever is driving ties me down before taking off. It's a good thing rugged individ-ualism isn't high on my list of personal virtues, since I can't purchase even a can of soup or a pair of socks by myself.

Although I can move for short distances over grass or gravel, I'm pretty well confined to asphalt or cement. And let's face it, pavements are not an essentially west-ern phenomenon. True, quite a few western writers (like the majority of western residents) live in cities, and some even write about the urban spectacle, but the

West of our hearts remains untracked wilderness. Most of the West, therefore, lies beyond my range. I can travel into the countryside as far as a car will carry me, and after that I can only look. In some state and national parks, paved paths now wind from parking lots into gentle terrain, and this access is better than none at all. But the paths are, of necessity, short; I can't wander off if a blossom or an insect intrigues me (nor can plants or creatures be persuaded to come present themselves for scrutiny); and at the end I must always stop and look out into a landscape closed to me absolutely and forever. This is the quintessential western posture—gaze ever longing into the beyond—stripped of its attendant capacity to act out the eyes' desire.

There is much to be said for looking, and I've gotten good at it, maybe better than most people whose vigorous strides alter their perspective distractingly. But it is not adequate compensation. I know. Though never an athlete, I was once an enthusiastic walker, who could stop and look, as deeply as I liked, whenever I felt like it *and then move on.* I can no longer move on, and sometimes I think I will die of grief at the loss. Or rather, I can move on only in imagination and so, in an odd way, I've come full circle, back to my eastern childhood when I envisioned steamy fireside encounters for my novel-commissioner, Sal. Now, left behind from a family camping trip, I visualize the adventure they later recount: the bears, mother and son, consulting each other in deep mumbles as they pried at the windows of my daughter's brand-new car while she and her husband

and her father peered apprehensively from their tent until Eric, ever the Boy Scout, banged together the pot lids he had armed himself with at bedtime and the astonished bears shambled away.

Not just looking and listening, and certainly not imagining, but *moving* constitutes the western experience, however, and in such terms I can never become a western writer. It would strike some as an odd ambition anyhow. Most writers, except possibly southern ones, resist a regional label, believing that their work ought to have "broad," even "universal" appeal. Modesty is not generally a writer's strong suit. Nor is it mine, so why would I want to lay claim to a reductive label suggesting that I write books about rootless rugged individuals tearing through (and up) a landscape fit only for cattle and rattlesnakes and an occasional shootout at some good enough corral? This sketch does not represent the work of most western writers today, but it does reflect the common and still current interpretation of "western."

If that interpretation really reflected what a western writer is, I wouldn't want to be one. I don't want to confine myself to a parochial category, especially one that bears no discernible relation to my real work. I want to expand that category to its fullest possible extent. Attribute this, if you will, to a westerner's predilection for wide-open spaces.

"Mobility" really was once a necessary element of life in the West. I could not have survived here as an Anasazi cliff dweller, a colonial settler at a mission or hacienda, a Mormon pioneer hauling my worldly goods to Utah in a handcart, a Bisbee miner's wife. I needed to wait for pavement, for cities—and not just any city, not Bisbee, for instance, or San Francisco or Seattle, but a city on a plain, in a valley, warm and dry, too, since my wheelchair doesn't sport an umbrella or snow tires. Such cities exist now, have existed for decades, among them my personal favorites, Tucson and Los Angeles. The high-rise concrete cliff dwellings of Century City are as authentically western as the stone cliff dwellings of Mesa Verde (in geographical terms, several hundred miles more so), only they have elevators instead of ladders, a difference that means the world to me.

So, I would argue, easy mobility, like rootlessness and rugged individualism, is no longer essential to the western experience. They are anachronisms that should be discarded from the way we imagine the West. But the danger is that in removing such strictures, I'll render "western" too indistinct to be meaningful, and I don't intend at all to suggest that the West contains nothing that peculiarly sets those of us who write in and about it apart from our scribbling cousins in Boston, Baltimore, and Baton Rouge. On the contrary, there is plenty peculiar about the place: more, in fact, than conventional critics deign to notice.

The basic realities haven't changed. There is, for example, the matter of magnitude. "The sky is bigger out here," I told my mother back in Enon shortly after I'd moved to the desert, and she replied in the tone she's always used to deflate my grander fancies: "Oh, don't be silly. The sky is the same size everywhere." "The sky," she confessed on her first visit a few months later, "is bigger out here." And so therefore is the land stretched out beneath it. From the mountains north of Tucson it is possible on a fine day to see all the way into Mexico, about eighty miles to the south. Living in the midst of such space, especially when it was empty of any human sign, a newcomer might have had difficulty stopping and staying put, and he certainly could have suffered the delusion that he had the place, all of it, to himself.

Some may respond the same way today. But not everybody. The immensity remains constant—it is intrinsically western—but the range of responses to it has grown with the population. Some may still see in it the chance to flee the past and start fresh and/or to grow rich gouging out or hacking down or grazing off its resources, but they (both the people and the resources) grow fewer with time. Many now view it as a giant playground to be grassed over with golf courses and pocked with swimming pools and scoured with dune buggies and dirt bikes. Some are threatened, others soothed. A few may take it, as I must, as chastisement: a vastness within which my yearning spirit must grapple with my recalcitrant flesh perpetually.

The West teems with implacable realities—too little water where too many people insist on settling; a series of faults that threaten to dump the nation's most glorious real estate into the drink; two long international borders and an even longer coastline across which flow people, drugs, and weather systems to destabilize the status quo—and plenty of transitory realities as well, like grunge rock and incendiary religious cults. Insofar as any writing is shaped, either implicitly or explicitly, by its engagement with any of these, the writer can lay claim to the West.

"No, not *that* story," say a couple of editors who have asked me to write about how the West has shaped me when I send them these reflections on the difficulties I have encountered in claiming an identity as a chronicler of the West. "That's not at all what we have in mind." To clarify, they give me examples of what they do have in mind, pieces built around backwoodspersons and long reflective walks by the verges of isolated lakes, about the uses of firearms and childhood encounters with Indians; and I can tell that they want me to write a story essentially like other women's stories with the trifling but possibly intriguing difference that I happen to experience whatever befalls me at the height of those women's belt buckles.

But that's not the way disability works. It does not leave one precisely the same woman one would have been without it, only (in my case) shorter. It does not merely alter a few, or even a great many, details in a life story that otherwise conforms to basic narrative conventions: the adventure, the romance, the quest. Instead, it transforms the tale utterly, though often subtly, and these shifts in narrative tone and type arouse resistance in both the "author" and the "reader" of the outlandish plot.

These disparities have had their consequences, for me and for those who have shared my misshapen life, many of which were encapsulated several years ago when my husband, my daughter, and I made a pass through this overlarge landscape in what we recall, with no fondness whatsoever, as the Camper from Hell. Anne, just out of college, was soon to join the Peace Corps and spend a couple of years in Zaïre, and she wanted to travel in the Southwest before leaving it, perhaps for good. On expeditions in earlier years, we had wandered from campground to campground with an increasingly shabby but serviceable Eureka Space 10 tent, sleeping bags, and air mattresses; but although I was still able to walk short distances, and getting down on the ground was all too easy for me, getting me up again was a group production none of us looked forward to; and so we rented, as cheaply as possible, a camper with a kitchenette, beds, and a toilet.

In hindsight, "as cheaply as possible" turned out to be the falsest of economies. We didn't have any money— we've never had any money—but if we had it to do over again, George and I would probably take a second mortgage on the house rather than search out that dubious director of a rundown nursery school and rent his infernal camper for a week's tour of New Mexico. We should have been wary when the camper wasn't ready as promised; but, as Anne would no doubt be glad to attest, George and I have always been deficient in the wariness department.

We loaded hastily and left just a little behind schedule, which would turn out to be our condition throughout the trip, arriving at our first campground, in Alamo-gordo, well after dark. There we discovered that the water in the camper's tanks stank sulfurously and the mechanism for converting the dining benches into one of the beds was so broken that the bed could be created only with great wrenchings and swearings. These I could not participate in, but the least I could do was volunteer to sleep on the outcome, a mound of lumpen upholstery whose metal frame poked my back and hips no matter which way I twisted. Since I wasn't doing any driving, I didn't think George or Anne ought to spend their nights tossing about à la The Princess and the Pea.

At Carlsbad the next night, the pump for the sulfurous water, which had been working only sporadically, quit entirely. In the morning we found someone to replace the water pump, but we couldn't start out for Santa Fe until after lunch, too long a trip, it turned out, so that we had trouble locating our campground north of the city in the dark. In the mountains miles to the north of Taos the next night, George hit a tree in the dark and banged up the camper, though he resisted the urge to finish the damned thing off. In the morning it retaliated by refusing to start altogether, and George had to call the owner, who seemed eerily familiar with the problem and issued elaborate instructions involving many hands and feet and bits of paper.

All along, our primary object had been a return to a place Anne had loved ten years or more before, Chaco Canyon, which didn't look too far from Taos on the map. But of course maps don't show you ways of getting lost on the hills across which Los Alamos is scattered or roads so steep that the wheezing camper won't chug over ten miles an hour. The scenery was breathtaking, especially a huge empty green valley enclosed on every side by mountains up to ten thousand feet high. But it was already getting dark when we reached Cuba, a town so derelict as to seem a parody of the rural West rather than a habitable community. Here Anne suddenly burst out that she was having a terrible time and had not enjoyed a single thing—not the dunes at White Sands where she and her father had romped, or the ribbon of bats silvery in the dusk above Carlsbad Caverns, or even the fry bread heaped with beans, meat, lettuce, tomatoes, cheese, and salsa, very tasty and messy, eaten before an audience of four hungry but mannerly dogs on a log in a plaza at Pueblo de Taos—and wanted to head straight home without bothering with Chaco Canyon at all.

She'd been moody all along, and with more reason than even the Camper from Hell provided. She wasn't feeling well, and she was still very upset about the loss, during a burglary of our house a few days before we set out, of an irreplaceable heirloom ring her great-grandmother had just given her for college graduation. Moreover, she'd be leaving home and friends in another month to begin training for two years of service in Africa. And then there was the bitter though unacknowledged reality that the camper was not the only dilapidated and malfunctioning entity on this trip, no moment of which could be truly carefree.

The trip provided endless exercises in problem-solving and sheer brute force: hunting for accessible parking spaces, toilets, walkways; hauling me and then the wheelchair out of the vehicle and later stowing us both again; and in between incessant pushing, tilting, swerving, pushing, pushing, pushing, pushing. No one could forget for more than an instant that I am a cripple. Of course, I could be parked and left, but then the leaver had to deal with feelings of guilt or loneliness or dread of returning to me and so was still not wholly free. Whatever we managed to do—and thanks to modifications of terrain or architecture, we often did a lot—was tinged with the kind of regret I had felt a few days earlier at Carlsbad Caverns, wishing we could have hiked in instead of plunging 750 feet straight down in an elevator. Still, most of the inside trail was wheelchair accessible, so I'd gotten to see a good bit, though in considerable discomfort, since Anne whipped the wheelchair along at breakneck speed. This is one of the means she has used to punish me for my illness and dependency, though I don't think she has ever known it. Sometimes George too, intentionally though unconsciously, hurts me when he is "helping" me, but not so frequently. I try not to complain at such times, not because I'm a martyr but because I think they need this sort of outlet for their anger, which I share.

That's how the Camper from Hell was functioning, too. Anne's fury at my disease (which is not quite the same as fury at me, though the fact that I bear the disease in my flesh renders this distinction problematic) defied direct expression, but it could safely be projected upon our rattling, stinking, hiccoughing conveyance, along with the other griefs and terrors currently plaguing her. I sympathized. But I was also getting sick of tiptoeing every minute to avoid a new attack of ill temper, and I surprised myself by insisting that we stop for something to eat and talk our situation over before planning our next move. Confrontation has never been my style.

So we found a cafe. Anne ordered cauliflower soup, which had the consistency and color (and perhaps flavor—I didn't ask) of library paste, and a glob of cottage cheese floating in the middle of a plate of canned fruit cocktail. George and I had chef's salads, iceberg lettuce with gristly bits of beef and ham and some slices of pasteurized processed cheese food. Over this dismal repast we talked and wept and finally resolved to spend the night in a motel, get the engine checked in the morning, then go to Chaco as planned and from there home. Dinner ended with a soggy three-way hug in the middle of the cafe, which no doubt turned some Cuban heads. So for just over a quarter of the hundred dollars we'd saved by leasing the Camper from Hell instead of a new one at a dealership, we rented a shabby but clean enough room in the Cuba Lodge Motel, watched a rerun of "Upstairs, Downstairs" and the news, and got some sleep.

I wish I could say that after this imbroglio, no further disasters marred our progress toward home. We would reach Tucson, it turned out, in one piece and more or less speaking to each other. But first there were the miles and miles of washboard road into and then out of Chaco, over which the camper jittered and bucked, raising billows of choking dust, until we were dizzy and bruised. There was the primitive campground in Navajo, arrived at late of course, where George accidently stuck the electrical cord into an unmarked 220 outlet (which shouldn't have been there) and melted the plug, so that our final stop was suitably benighted. We were limp with more than relief by the time we wound through the Salt River Canyon, rounded the Catalinas, and dropped into the Santa Cruz Valley we had left— could it have been?—only seven days before.

At the time, I half wished that we had stayed there and seen to our responsibilities rather than traipsing off to squander a lot of money and our spirits as well. But I also knew that nothing is ever entirely a waste. Visions of dunes carved against searing blue, of glassy cave pools, of a mother pronghorn with her twins behind her, of the little earthen plaza at Tesuque Pueblo, of the gash in the earth's skin carved by the Rio Grande outside Taos, of low mountains striated with rose and lavender and sage, of a precipitous rock stairway hacked a thousand years ago into a canyon wall: all would stay vivid and cherishable forever. The camper we could hurriedly return to its smarmy owner, pushing its memory back, down, behind these lovelier images.

The camper's bodily analogue could not be similarly banished, however, and so this trip has remained colored, as so many of my stories are now, by rage and disappointment. Why then don't I find the master plot a sad one? And I don't. The recollection of Anne and Nancy, blond head and brown head bowed, boohooing aloud while their tears splash onto picked-over fruit cocktail and lettuce, and even George swiping at his eyes with a crumpled paper napkin, strikes me as poignant but comic. The story of my life is certainly spoiled, in the sense sociologist Erving Goffman had in mind in subtitling his study of stigma *Notes on the Management of Spoiled Identity*, but it is far from ruined. It is merely radically unconventional.

The tale of westward migration has always been premised on possibility: gold hidden in the next black hill, endlessly fertile soil for wheat and grapes and artichokes, vast tracts of rangeland for sleek white-faced cattle, and eighteen holes of golf every day of the sun-drenched year. I moved into a West of impossibility. The East would be just as forbidding today, but that doesn't matter, since the East I have in mind is the land of childhood and perfectly inaccessible anyway. I moved into an adulthood that I, like other dreamers of the conventional West, could never have conceived: the strangest of lands. Nevertheless, though instead of loping on Old Paint across the lone prairie, I may be heading my Quickie P100 on down the alley and out to Bentley's for an iced cappuccino, it's an honest-to-God western adventure I'm having here.

Into the Wider World

IN AIRPORTS I break down and weep. Other venues provoke me to passion of various disagreeable sorts: indignation when someone without a handicapped license plate has taken a reserved space; frustration when a shop crowds in so much merchandise that I can't get my wheelchair down the aisles without risk of smothering in racks of finery or knocking down elaborate displays of fragile items; impatience when I'm trapped on the wrong side of an unautomated door that nobody else in the world seems inclined to go through; panic and, ironically, loneliness when large gatherings of people in enclosed spaces, like theatre audiences, mill around me, waving and calling out to each other, without ever glancing down. I grow aloof. I grow grim. At odd moments I blurt out something embarrassingly rude. But for the most part I remain in control. Only airports send me straight over the emotional top.

Part of the problem has nothing to do with being crippled, I suspect. I loathe upheaval of any sort, and I wouldn't find myself in an airport if I weren't about to engage in the most disruptive activity ever devised: travel. I don't want to be here. I want to go home. I want to sit, silent and solitary, in my studio. At 7:00 I want to go into the house and watch "The NewsHour with Jim Lehrer" while I eat my dinner. I want to sleep in my own bed, with my own little black cat between my knees and the machine that masks neighborhood noises as it thrums in imitation of a night train ferrying me across the continent of the dark to a day as nearly identical as I can make it to the one just past. *Local* travel: that's all I want.

Aside from my distaste for change, I seem largely immune to the free-floating anxieties that plague many travelers. I am not, like my husband, haunted by the conviction that I've left the stove on and the house is burning down. Nor am I, like my daughter, a white-knuckle flier. I do not believe, like my mother-in-law, that I am going to get lost and spend the rest of my days wandering, oddly invisible and thus beyond rescue, through the purgatorial reaches of O'Hare. My anxiety, specific and acute, relates almost solely to my physical helplessness, which is—since we travel with a lightweight, collapsible manual wheelchair—virtually complete. Without my batteries, I can't move an inch: my personal version of amputation.

Thus vulnerable, I find my treatment by the airlines downright crazy-making. Unlike bus and rail services, airlines are exempt from the Americans with Disabilities Act. Falling instead under the earlier and less stringent Air Carriers Access Act, they are basically free to do with disabled passengers what they will. There are no uniform policies among airlines, nor is any individual airline self-consistent. When, for instance, I've requested ahead of time seats in the first row of coach class, which have extra space in front of them, I've been told, "We can't give those out until you get to the airport," only to be told at the ticket counter on arrival, "Oh, we gave those out months ago." What actually happens to me—whether I get a bulkhead seat, whether my wheelchair is permitted into the cabin with me as formally required on flights of more than a hundred passengers, and so forth—depends not upon regulations but upon the whim of the individual agent.

On occasion, this fluidity can operate in our favor. On one flight from Dallas to London, the gate agent, dissatisfied with our seat assignment in the thirty-eighth row of coach, chosen because it placed me relatively close to the lavatories, bumped us up to the fifth row of first class, where we ate and drank our way across the Atlantic: champagne before departure; caviar with chopped onion, hard-cooked egg, and sour cream (we declined the accompanying vodka); cold lobster with herbed mayonnaise; green salad with Dijon vinaigrette; grapefruit sorbet; bouillabaise with a nice Chardonnay; coffee and Godiva chocolates; Drambuie. But wait, I haven't finished! After watching *Arachnophobia* on our individual little screens and dozing for a couple of hours in our deeply padded seats with footrests raised, it was time to eat again: papaya and strawberries; grapefruit juice; coffee; yogurt with muesli; croissant with marmalade. We turned down the cooked-to-order eggs. And then, as though worried that we'd starve once turned loose in the wilds of England, our flight attendant pressed on us two bottles of champagne, more chocolates, and travel kits containing such necessities as Evian atomizers and Hermès body lotion. We waddled off the plane at Gatwick in a sybaritic stupor.

Without my MS, we would never have had this luxury. We certainly weren't about to pay for it, and anyway, it wouldn't have been the same if we had. Part of the bliss derived from its sheer egregiousness: We hadn't expected it; we'd done nothing to merit it; we would never have it again. All the same, I find dependence on the whim of airline personnel so nerve-wracking that I'd sooner sit in steerage and eat dreaded turkey-and-cheese sandwiches (which we were once served six times within a single month) if only I could be guaranteed an accessible seat.

Here's the drill: We arrive at an airport and George loads me into the manual Pogon chair. When I was still able to travel alone, I used to take my Amigo scooter, but the airlines screwed it up so many times that I've never dared trust them with my beloved Quickie power chair. As soon as we've checked our bags, we rush to an agent to see whether we can change our inevitably terrible seats. Then through security, where I must wait until a female agent is available to pat me down, because I can't go through the electronic gate with my chair. A stop at the women's room, into which George pushes me with practiced sang-froid even when an outraged attendant scolds him, before arriving at the gate in plenty of time for early boarding.

I have never understood why people stampede to board a plane; as one who is always first on and last off, I should think they'd want to spend the least possible time in the cramped, stale space where I've logged so many idle hours. Nevertheless, I get some envious and occasionally resentful stares as the gate agent whisks me down the jetway with George in tow. If by some miracle we've actually secured bulkhead seats, in most planes I can toddle (this sounds cuter than it looks) to them with George walking ahead, turned backward, holding my arms to keep me erect; he dumps me unceremoniously into my seat and races back to fold the Pogon before a baggage handler, unfamiliar with its odd design, can wrench and jam it. If not seated in the bulkhead, I have to transfer on the jetway and be strapped to a narrow aisle chair, which two of the ground crew then roll to one of the back rows; since the arms of these seats seldom lift out of the way, they then heave me up over the arm and into the seat, very like a side of beef or a sack of grain. At least, now that virtually all airports have jetways, I no longer have to be loaded aboard on a forklift. Still, by this time I've been so jerked around, in every sense of the phrase, that I'm often sniffling with exhaustion and exasperation.

/ / /

Good grief, I can hear you saying about now, *why ever do you go through this rigmarole if it upsets you so?* I'm no masochist. I detest pain and refuse to endure any preventable form unless some other factors outweigh it. In this case, one of these is that a writer's life is, paradoxically, at once sedentary and itinerant. I sit still for long hours to compose a book, but then I'm expected to take the finished project on the road: to book-signings, high-school and college classes, conferences, public readings around the country. Some writers refuse this task altogether and others perform it grudgingly; but since I've chosen to live in relative seclusion at the farthest reaches of the civilized world (as was made plain to me by the *New York Times* editor who, having waked me with a telephone call at seven in the morning, seemed stunned at the notion that any place could have a time zone *three hours* earlier than Manhattan's), I welcome the opportunity to interact with audiences, whose images I can carry home with me and project onto the blank blue eye of my computer screen to remind me who I'm writing for.

For some years I was able to manage these trips on my own without serious misadventure, though one September, during a week at the University of Wyoming, my Amigo summarily gave up moving in reverse (and one of life's sterner laws is that you can't travel forward unless you can also back up). Several frantic telephone calls bore out my suspicion: no repair shop in Laramie seemed ever to have heard of an electric scooter. Fortunately, a fan who had heard I was coming somehow

tracked me down in my room (no chance of going anywhere else, and anyway, it was *snowing* outside) and,
upon hearing my tale of woe, lent me her scooter for the
remainder of my visit.

Now that I can no longer dress myself, traveling alone
to any destination other than a nudist colony is impractical, and so George uses family sick leave to accompany me, transforming business trips into a kind of
holiday. Mishaps still occur, of course. When my wheelchair, bruised by careless baggage handlers, disinte-
grated on the brick sidewalks of Beacon Hill, George
had to make an unexpected taxi run to a pharmacy at
the Boston University Hospital to rent another for a few
days—but somehow we always cope.

Another factor that persuades me to undertake travel's rigors is the conviction, born of experience, that no
matter what happens, once I get home again, I will have
had a terrific time. Our trip to Zaïre for Christmas 1988
proved this once and for all. We'd never been abroad before, and Africa didn't strike us as an ideal location for a
trial run, but that's where our daughter was. The Peace
Corps simply doesn't post people to Frankfurt or Zu-
rich, where we sojourned for a night on our way to and
from Kinshasa. One of the blessings that comes with pa-
rental territory is that children tug you into experiences
you're pretty sure you'd never otherwise contemplate. I
finally found a travel agent who looked upon planning a
trip for a cripple into the Heart of Darkness as a challenge; we spent the entire autumn getting inoculated
against one horrific disease after another; and a couple

of days before Christmas we were as ready as we were likely to get. "Everything will be fine as long as we don't get sick," George said as we lay sleepless the night before our departure. "You can't have any fun if you're puking your guts out."

A few days later, as he was engaged in precisely this activity, I reminded him of his words. "Well, I was wrong," he gasped between heaves. "I'm having a wonderful time." He was sincere. Not that he was enjoying this gastric catastrophe. Whatever he had picked up was a very bad bug indeed, which took him some weeks to get rid of. But everything about life in this whitewashed, tin-roofed bungalow at the edge of the forest, lit by candles and kerosene lanterns, with goats and chickens and small giggling children wandering in and out, was so fresh and fascinating to us that even being sick here elated him. After a day or so, ample infusions of Pepto Bismol and Gatorade restored him sufficiently that he could rejoin the activities that Anne had planned. He and Anne's little dog Celeste even chased down one of her chickens to provide our farewell feast, though when the time arrived, he could stomach only rice. When we departed on Epiphany, he believed as fervently as I that the trip represented the high point of our quarter of a century together.

In hindsight, Africa may have been ideal for our maiden international venture after all. When I was getting ready to go to England for the first time in 1990, I said to Anne, who had recently returned from Zaïre via Kenya, Egypt,

and England, "You know, it's odd but I don't feel especially nervous about this trip."

"Mother, you've been to *Africa*," she retorted. "England is nothing!"

England is not actually nothing. For me, it is a bound-
less source of delight. Indeed, if the climate weren't so
foul (one June when we were there, a hard frost killed
half the strawberry crop), I'd probably do a T. S. Eliot
move. In terms of traveling with a disability, however,
England presents remarkably few obstacles. If in the
United States my special needs are frequently met with
a slightly aggrieved air, as though I had adopted a wheelchair solely to harass sales clerks, ticket agents, and taxi
drivers, the English are, by contrast, solicitous and even
a little apologetic, as though it really had been most inconsiderate of William the Conqueror and his comrades
at arms to use so many steps in their castles but I must
at least be able to get into the gardens and feed the
swans.

Not that we're immune to calamity there, of course.
As long as we have my body—especially my quirky
bladder—along, we're bound to get into scrapes of one
sort or another. One night we found ourselves in rather
dire straits—George having rolled me over rough sidewalks, for what only seemed like hours, in search of a
toilet—suddenly in front of the Savoy Hotel. One of the
high points of George's father's eighty years had been
taking tea here a year or so before he died. I imagined
how mortified he'd have been at our approaching the
place at this hour, for this purpose. Although we have

seldom been treated less than cordially in England, the doorman at the Savoy was downright frosty to these uncouth Americans straggling in from the Strand in search of an available convenience, accessible or not, really anything would do. Tersely, he issued a set of instructions of astounding complexity, involving two different elevators, the first of which opened (whether by his intention or our misinterpretation we could not be sure) upon an enormous mound of very smelly refuse, truly the entrails of the Savoy. Backtracking and casting about through long featureless corridors lined by closed doors, at last we achieved our goal, and not a moment too soon.

Emergencies of this variety have occurred less frequently since we learned of an indispensable key issued by RADAR (the Royal Association for Disability and Rehabilitation). Virtually every English town has public toilets, including a separate facility, spacious and well-equipped, for people with disabilities and their caregivers, which can be opened only by RADAR key. I don't leave home without it.

Strategic planning is, of course, imperative for all travelers who choose to tailor their excursions to their own needs and interests rather than join a packaged tour, especially if the exigencies of disability are added into the equation. George and I start daydreaming and gathering information, through letters and telephone calls, months in advance. Once we've arranged in detail for lodging and transportation, we are ready to let our day-to-day experiences—the disasters and disappointments as well as the delights—unfold. We rely on serendipity for much of our fun.

On our first trip to England, we spent five days in London and then rented a car for another five days in the countryside. Our route through the Cotswolds from Stratford to Bath took us through Willersey, with a swan pond on one side of the road, a pub called The Bell on the other, complete with an actual bell out front, and a stone church on a hill above. Enchanted, we left our wretched little Vauxhall in the car park behind the pub; and as we made our way slowly up the narrow lane toward the perpendicular-style steeple visible through the trees, we encountered clusters of people in black coming down. Sure enough, there was a freshly dug grave, now deserted except for the gravedigger, in the churchyard at the top. We spent some time in the empty church, a stone-chill but graceful space that had kept—miraculously after the heavy bombing of World War II—some of its fourteenth-century windows, before heading back down in search of some lunch at The Bell.

"We've only cold food," the publican told us. "We've all been at a funeral."

"Yes, we gathered," we said. "Sandwiches will be fine." As we sat among the mourners, munching our bread and cheese and sipping our bitter, we concurred in our desire to enter village life more deeply: "We must come back here and stay."

This is how, a year later, we found ourselves in a converted cow byre not exactly in Willersey but in another picturesque Cotswold village, Stretton-on-Fosse, which had its own St. Peter's, even colder and not as pretty as the one that had lured us back but close enough, close enough. We had begun to plan our return, this time with my parents to share both adventures and expenses, almost as soon as we got to Tucson, getting so far as to collect catalogues from several agencies that handle rentals of cottages in the English countryside, circling the few marked "suitable for the disabled" and permitting ourselves to dream. Then, in December, a six-centimeter melanoma was removed from George's belly. The catalogues were swept into a file drawer, and we began to prepare for a different journey altogether.

He seemed unlikely to live for very long, but when he rallied remarkably well from massive surgery, the oncologist suggested that we try some chemotherapy. For three days every three weeks, chemicals of unimaginable toxicity dripped into his veins; and although the short-term side effects were hideous, he began visibly to gain weight and grow stronger. By April he was speaking again of traveling to England. "Oh, no," Dr. Jackson said when we broached the subject. "Absolutely not. Out of the question. I don't want you more than a day away. Maybe a cabin in the Chiricahuas, but certainly not a cottage in the Cotswolds." Although, admittedly, London is more hours distant from Tucson by plane than the Chiricahua Mountains are by car, the trip still takes less than a day. But you sometimes have to give your doctor time to adjust to an idea.

We said nothing for a couple of weeks. When we

raised the question again, his refusal seemed less ada-
mant. We waited a little longer, until we really had to
get our plans in order if we were going to go at all. I telephoned him and asked again. "Well, Nancy, we're not
going to cure this guy, so we have to consider quality of
life." These were not comforting words, but I could
smell capitulation. "If it's really important to him, go
ahead." One week after his sixth and final round of chemotherapy, we were on our way. Although still weak
and easily fatigued, he drove 1179 miles, all on the
wrong side of the road, and pushed my wheelchair
through castles and cathedrals, car parks and formal
gardens, ruined abbeys, woollen mills, and the full cir-
cuit of Stonehenge in a bitter wet wind. On our return
to Tucson two weeks later, he was more vigorous than
when we had left. Although I don't think that England
can claim true curative qualities, the fact is that, for
reasons no one has been able to fathom, George got
well. England seems as good a reason for his recupera-
tion as any.

A country cottage turned out to suit us perfectly. By settling in one spot in the countryside, from which we can
make day trips, rather than moving from hotel to hotel
in order to cover a large area, we can unpack and pack
just once; we can prepare some of our own meals; and if
we don't feel up to an outing, we have a "home" to stay
at instead of being cooped up in one room. More important, we are immersed in the local scene as we attend
the parish church, shop at nearby markets, watch inter-

minable and incomprehensible but oddly mesmerizing cricket matches on the village green, and hang out in the nearest pub. There are thousands of cottages (and even an occasional castle) available as rentals, sleeping from two to a dozen or more, throughout the British Isles; and a few of these are described as "suitable for the disabled." Because no single definition of "disabled" covers all conditions, the exact nature of this suitability may vary, however, as we discovered at the "accessible" hotel in Bristol, on our first trip, which had "only" six steps between our room and the dining room.

On our 1994 trip, we and our parents rented a handsomely converted pony stable (what next, I wonder: a pig sty? a dove cote?) with a glorious private garden in the village of West Peckham, near Maidstone, in Kent. Much care had been taken to adapt both house and garden for a wheelchair user, and the result was nearly ideal except that the toilet was too low for me to transfer without assistance. There was no plastic riser, the owner said, because their disabled guests had always driven from some other part of England, bringing their own with them. "We've never had an intrepid international traveler like you," she laughed. Nevertheless, a plastic riser would be a good thing to have on hand, she decided briskly in what I've come to think of as the typical British manner, and first thing next morning, off she went to buy one.

Settled into a cottage, we can begin to poke around the countryside. On our first two trips, we had only the

Pogon to aid us. Since propelling this with me in it demands considerable exertion (especially after I've consumed cream teas for a week or so), and since if my pusher takes off on some errand of his own, I'm left stranded, I longed to motivate myself. Before the third trip, we discovered Trevor Pollitt of Wheelchair Travel, who has a fleet of lift-equipped minibuses, each complete with an Orange Badge, which permits parking almost everywhere, and the all-important RADAR key. Trevor had also arranged the rental of a power chair, so George and I were both truly—albeit sporadically—freer than before.

After a couple of days, we could tell that the batteries weren't charging, and eventually I ground to an ignominious halt. Back to the Pogon until Trevor could bring another to me. Within hours, this one went berserk. It would sink into catatonia, refusing to respond when I pressed the joystick, then without warning leap forward, not necessarily, or even very often, in the direction I was pointing it. It was thus potentially deadly to any person or thing within about a six-foot radius. Back to the Pogon. The rental agency having no more to offer, Trevor purchased a used chair outright and brought that to me. A couple of days later, a tire went flat with a spectacular whoosh. Fortunately our landlords knew of a cycle shop, and after a day for repair, this last chair served me admirably. It even had an ingenious set of rockers on the front, unlike anything I'd seen before, which enabled me to leap curbs.

/ / /

What has surprised us, on all three of our visits to England, is the number of places, many of them centuries old, which have been adapted to welcome the wheelchair traveler. Of course, the English eagerness to accommodate can sometimes get in the way of accuracy, as when we were told that we'd need just a little help, readily provided, getting into Ragley Hall. When we arrived at this imposing manor house, we confronted a flight of at least twenty steps; two burly gardeners were summoned to carry me in my wheelchair up and later down.

Helpfulness extends, we inadvertently discovered, even to the nobility. At Blenheim Palace, having already pushed me a considerable distance from the car park, George encountered a wooden ramp laid at a dangerous incline over the long flight of steps to the front entrance. Just then, a station wagon pulled into the courtyard and a family got out. "This ramp is much too steep," George said to them. "Could you give me a hand pushing the wheelchair up?" Although they looked a little startled, they obliged. Only later, upon learning that the Duke and Duchess of Marlborough were in residence, did we realize who we must have pressed into service.

Except at some private houses, disabled visitors, and sometimes their companions too, are generally admitted for a reduced fee or none at all. I attended both *Shirley Valentine* in London and *Twelfth Night* in Stratford without charge. In the United States, only the National Park Service offers free admission; anywhere else, although discounts for senior citizens are common, if you ask about provisions for disabled patrons (and I do ask, regularly, figuring it can't hurt to sow the seed), you are met with blank or even affronted stares. I can't quite fathom the difference between the countries, although I've wondered whether England's immersion this century in two harrowing wars, in which a much larger proportion of people were killed or maimed than in this country, helps to account for it.

For some reason, at any rate, the English attitude seems to be that infirmity, in and of itself, deserves compensation and solicitude. In the States, there is nothing meritorious about affliction. On the contrary, it is deemed shameful and at least a little suspect, as though one had become crippled on purpose and must be given as little consideration as possible lest one be tempted to suffer even more. I want to shake Charles Sykes, author of the querulous *A Nation of Victims*, and his ilk by the shoulders and shout: "*Look* at me. Do you think being like this is worth the paltry goodies society hands out? Do you really believe I'm enduring this so as to get a convenient parking spot and a ramp to the door? Do you think I prefer $6000 a year in disability payments to earning more than five times that much and enjoying collegiality and prestige as well? Do you think *anything* you could offer me would make up for MS? What are you, some kind of a nut?" In England, I'm not treated as though my nature would be utterly debauched by a free theatre ticket.

With George's connivance, I can sometimes achieve

—at least partially—the impossible. Here is his recollection of one such occasion, our visit to Monk's House in Rodmell

There's no way in, except through a gate and up four steps and follow the path around to the back and here's the entrance at last, through Leonard's greenhouse and down three steps.

"Isn't there some way in for a woman in an electric wheelchair?"

The man behind the table is slender, sixty-ish, strands of gray hair combed neatly across the top of his head. He smiles, wants to be helpful. But he says, "No. There just hasn't been a way for the Trust to ramp such a small building. They could do something with a castle, but not a private home like this. Sorry."

"Ahhhh! My wife is in an electric chair; she's a Woolf scholar. Has written about Woolf. She's out in the lane. We've come so far. From Tucson in the States. This is very important. We've come such a ways."

"No. You can see for yourself. There's no way in."

"What about the Trust flyer we read? It refers to limited access for the disabled. How can that be?" Now I am grasping. I'm not sure what the flyer does say. I may be lying. But he is thinking hard at this point.

"Well, it shouldn't say that. But wait. Up at the top of the garden there is an ancient gate, and I don't even know where the key is. Perhaps we could unlock the gate into the garden."

"Yes. If we could at least see the garden."

Nancy and I go up a yet narrower lane, really a paved footpath, running alongside the garden wall, to an ancient-appearing wooden door set in the wall. It's locked tight. Perhaps the key can't be found. A tall young man rushes up with the key. The gate is opened. He helps us through. No steps. The chair slews momentarily in a bit of mud, and then Nancy is in and on her way down the garden path.

From here I can actually peer into Virginia's studio, with the broad bare table at which she wrote, and her bedroom, the window above the narrow bed overlooking the misty downs, and I want no more.

All the good will in the world can't compensate completely for my limitations, of course, and so I've developed a traveling spirit that mingles resolve with resignation. I'll try every venture that looks feasible, taking whatever help I can get, but I've also learned to give up calmly, if not always cheerfully, in the face of impossibility. No matter how carefully we've planned, things will go wrong. No matter how obliging our English hosts, I'll sometimes be left out. I can't climb the tower at Warwick Castle, after all, and I certainly don't expect a lift to be installed, even if such a measure were practicable. The aerial view of the village will simply never be mine (but then, trembling with exhaustion at the top, my mother wasn't altogether glad it was hers).

At Knole, the 365-room ancestral home of the Sackvilles, only the oak-paneled Great Hall can be reached by wheelchair. I can huddle in it grieving over the rare and fabulous silver furniture the others will see upstairs in the King's Room without me. Or I can contemplate the ancestral portraits all around me, the elaborately ornamented oak screen at one end, and, when I've looked deeply enough, wheel out into the Green Court to bask in the rare bit of English sun, dreaming that Vita Sackville-West and Virginia Woolf once walked by this very spot, heads together, arms entwined, their laughter fluttering through the gate and out into the deer park beyond. Only one of these options will bring me joy.

I choose joy.

NOTES

PLUNGING IN

1. Erving Goffman, *Stigma: Notes on the Management of Spoiled Identity* (New York: Simon & Schuster, 1963), passim.

BODY IN TROUBLE

1. Erving Goffman, *Stigma: Notes on the Management of Spoiled Identity* (New York: Simon & Schuster, 1963), passim.

TAKING CARE

1. Judith Viorst, *Necessary Losses* (New York: Ballantine, 1986), p. 37.
2. John Hockenberry, *Moving Violations: War Zones, Wheelchairs, and Declarations of Independence* (New York: Hyperion, 1995), pp. 6, 5.
3. Hockenberry, p. 97.
4. Adrienne Asch, "Abused or Neglected Clients—or Abusive or Neglectful Service Systems?" in *Ethical Conflicts in the Management of Home Care: The Case Manager's Dilemma* (New York: Springer Publishing Company, 1993), pp. 118, 119.

OPENING DOORS

1. *Friendly Wheels* 21, no. 69 (fall 1994): 5.
2. Ironically, Tucson's system has actually been more progressive than ADA mandates, and so the city is currently *cutting it back* to meet ADA requirements.

WRITING WEST

1. Jackson J. Benson, "His Finest Work of Art Was Himself: Wallace Stegner, 1909–1993," *Center: The Magazine of PEN Center USA West* (Summer 1993): 15.
2. Deanne Stillman, "Again, That Hankering," *New York Times*, August 22, 1993, sec. 2, p. 20.